Sermons for Feasts, Festivals & Occasions

Sermons for

Feasts, Festivals & Occasions

Selections from
Concordia Pulpit
Resources

CONCORDIA PUBLISHING HOUSE · SAINT LOUIS

MORE SELECTIONS FROM CONCORDIA PULPIT RESOURCES

Sermons for Funerals, Weddings & Civil Holidays (15-5103)

Sermons for Advent and Christmas (15-5105)

Sermons for Lent and Easter (15-5106)

Copyright © 2008 Concordia Publishing House
3558 S. Jefferson Ave., St. Louis, MO 63118-3968
1-800-325-3040 • www.cph.org

Unless otherwise noted, Scripture quotations are from The Holy Bible, English Standard Version®. Copyright © 2001 by Crossway Bibles, a publishing ministry of Good News Publishers, Wheaton, Illinois. Used by permission. All rights reserved.

Scripture quotations marked NKJV™ are taken from the New King James Version®. Copyright © 1982 by Thomas Nelson, Inc. Used by permission. All rights reserved.

Hymn texts with the abbreviation *LSB* are from *Lutheran Service Book*, copyright © 2006 Concordia Publishing House. All rights reserved.

Material with the abbreviation *LSB Altar Book* is taken from *Lutheran Service Book: Altar Book*, copyright © 2006 Concordia Publishing House. All rights reserved.

Material with the abbreviation *TLH* is from *The Lutheran Hymnal*, copyright © 1941 Concordia Publishing House.

The quotations marked AE are from Luther's Works, American Edition: vols. 11, 21, and 22 copyright © 1976, 1956, 1957, respectively, by Concordia Publishing House. All rights reserved.

Quotations from the Lutheran Confessions in this publication are from *Concordia: The Lutheran Confessions*, second edition, copyright © 2006 Concordia Publishing House. All rights reserved.

Quotations marked *Luther's Small Catechism* taken from *Luther's Small Catechism with Explanation*, copyright © 1986, 1991 Concordia Publishing House.

Manufactured in the United States of America

Library of Congress Cataloging-in-Publication Data

Sermons for feasts, festivals, and occasions : selections from Concordia pulpit resources.
    p. cm.
    ISBN 978-0-7586-1378-3
    1. Occasional sermons. 2. Fasts and feasts—Sermons.
    3. Festivals—Sermons. 4. Lutheran Church—Sermons. I. Concordia pulpit
    resources. II. Title.
BV4254.2.S428 2008
252'.67—dc22

2007034387

1 2 3 4 5 6 7 8 9 10   17 16 15 14 13 12 11 10 09 08

Contents

Occasions

January

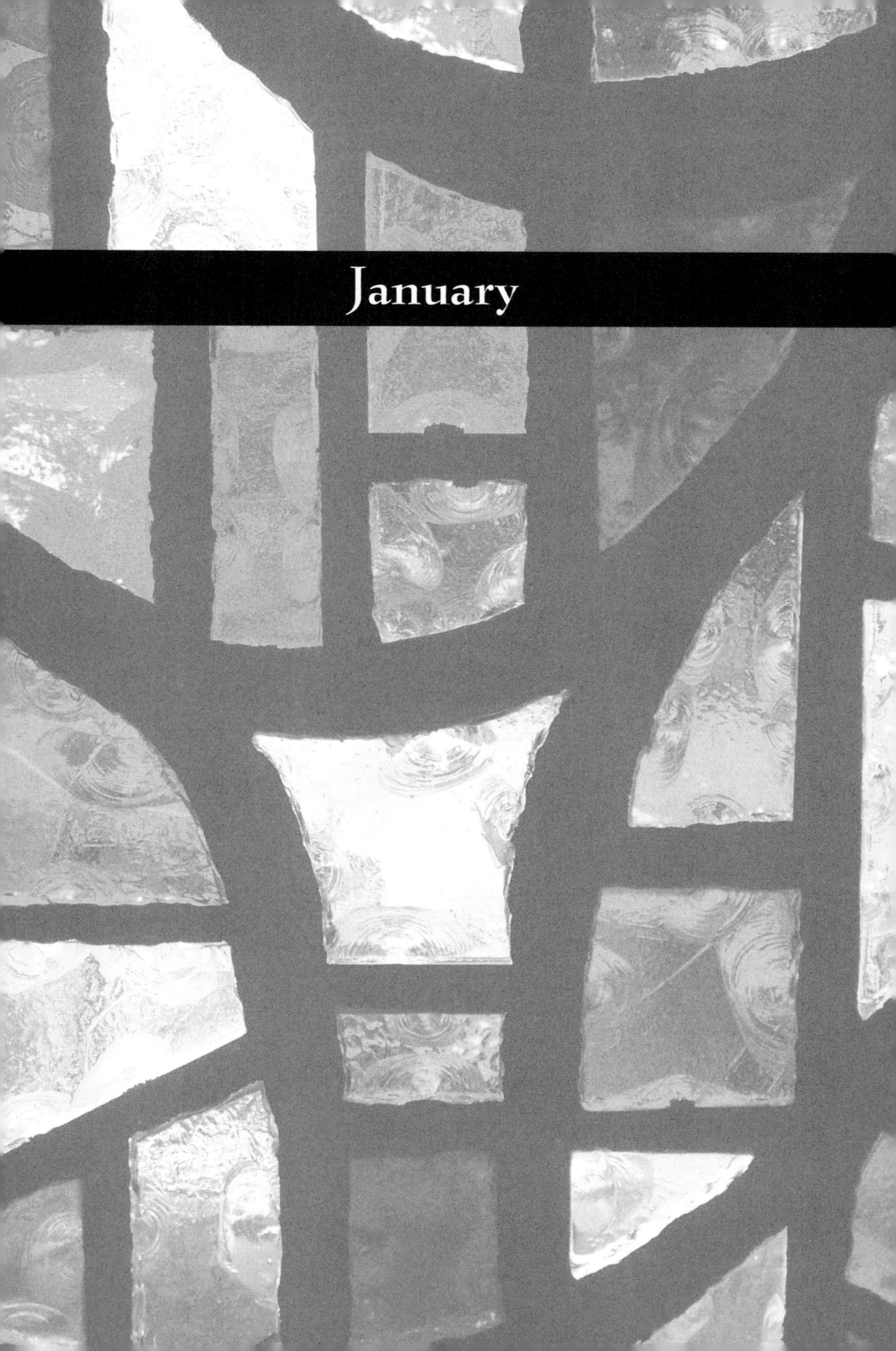

Circumcision and Name of Jesus

Two Timely Events

Luke 2:21

It is my birthday and we are going to go to the zoo. It is our anniversary and we are going out for dinner. On Thursday I will be released from the hospital and will be going home. This year on Memorial Day weekend we will be going to the Indy 500 race. On the Fourth of July we will be going to the riverfront to watch the fireworks. On Thanksgiving Day our family will all gather at John's folks for dinner. On Christmas Eve we will be opening our gifts after the family service.

Did you notice something consistent about each of the aforementioned statements? Each contained both a time frame and an event. First the day, the date, or the national holiday was indicated; you were given a specific time. Second, what would happen on that particular day was indicated. First the time, then the event.

The single verse appointed as the Gospel for New Year's Day does the same thing. But instead of one date and one event on that date, Luke tells us about two dates and two events—two timely events. The first time indicator is "at the end of eight days." The first event is Jesus' circumcision. The second time indicator is "before He was conceived." The second event is the giving of His name.

The text has yet more for us to take into account. Not only do we have two time frames, each coupled with an event, but, in fact, the two events are interrelated. On the same day Jesus is circumcised, He is also given His name.

As we begin this new year by honoring the name of our Lord through worship in His house, let's look more closely at these two events to appreciate just what God was doing on the eighth day of our Lord's earthly life. Immediately we realize that when God is at work among us, more is happening than meets the eye. Usually God is doing double duty. It may appear quite obvious that it is raining, but God is also causing the seed to grow as He waters the earth. God may permit trials and tribulations to enter our lives, but He is also strengthening our relationship with Him. God may allow disaster to befall those we love, but He is also giving us opportunity to minister to them. When one thing is happening to you, be sure to look for a second event that takes place simultaneously.

TIMING IS EVERYTHING: THE EIGHTH DAY

God's timing often coincides with our traditional timing, and vice versa. The eighth day (counting the day of birth) was the traditional day on which God commanded His covenant people to circumcise their male children. "He who is eight days old among you shall be circumcised" (Gen 17:12; cf. Lev 12:3).

God commanded the observance, and Mary and Joseph, devout in their faith, adhered to God's Law. "They had performed everything according to the Law of the Lord" (Lk 2:39). Already as an infant, Jesus was fulfilling the Law for us. The Lawgiver subjects Himself to the Law. "But when the fullness of time had come, God sent forth His Son, born of woman, born under the law, to redeem those who were under the law, so that we might receive adoption as sons" (Gal 4:4–5).

The eighth day was a significant holy day (holiday) for that individual and his family, the first week's anniversary of his birth.

THE TIME BEFORE JESUS WAS CONCEIVED

The angel appeared to Mary to announce that she was to be the mother of God's Son. "You will conceive in your womb" (Lk 1:31a).

The angel announced to Mary the name that should be given to this Son: "You shall call His name Jesus" (Lk 1:31b). Jesus means, "Yahweh (the LORD) is Savior." ("Yahweh" is the name of God repeated three times in the Benediction.) Matthew records, "You shall call His name Jesus, for He will save His people from their sins" (Mt 1:21).

The significance of His name is foretold: "He will be great and will be called the Son of the Most High. And the Lord God will give to Him the throne of His father David, and He will reign over the house of Jacob forever, and of His kingdom there will be no end" (Lk 1:32–33).

The conception is foretold: "The Holy Spirit will come upon you, and the power of the Most High will overshadow you; therefore the child to be born will be called holy—the Son of God" (Lk 1:35). Dr. Luke's special interest in the events surrounding the conception and birth of Jesus is reflected in his fuller account.

What time is it? We are just a few hours into the new year.

Are you cognizant of the timing when God chooses to be at work in your life through the ordinary events that take place day by day, hour by hour?

How has God used special holidays (holy days), birthdays, anniversaries, and so on, to do "double duty" among you?

God is cognizant of time and does His finest work with synchronized precision: "In the days of Herod, king of Judea" (Lk 1:5); "When [Zechariah's] time of service was ended" (Lk 1:23); "In the sixth month the angel Gabriel was sent from God to a city of Galilee named Nazareth" (Lk 1:26); "In those days Mary arose and went with haste" (Lk 1:39); "From now on all generations will call me blessed" (Lk 1:48). "Mary remained with her about three months" (Lk 1:56); "The time came for Elizabeth to give birth" (Lk 1:57); "In those days a decree went out from Caesar Augustus" (Lk 2:1).

Two Timely Events

The Child is circumcised. In humility Jesus subjected Himself to the Law of God. While His parents brought Him to be circumcised, Jesus, God in the flesh, permitted the painful circumcision. He was a true Israelite, Son of the covenant. He allowed His blood to be shed.

The child is named Jesus. The name means "Yahweh (the LORD) is Savior." This was the reassuring message given to Joseph: "You shall call His name Jesus, for He will save His people from their sins" (Mt 1:21).

As Savior, Jesus allows His blood to be shed. There is only one way to save people from their sins; the Lamb of God is sacrificed for the remission of their sins. There is only one whose blood is able to atone for the sins of all: the very Son of God, whose name is Jesus. There is only one who could shed all His blood for the sins of all and still live again—the Son of God. The two events, the circumcision and the naming of Jesus, are interrelated. The Son of God, whose earthly life included submitting to circumcision, sheds His blood as Savior to save us from our sins. The Son of God submitted to the Law of God (circumcision) and fulfilled the Law of God (in total) for us.

Because Jesus humbled Himself, allowed His blood to be shed, and fulfilled the Law, the Father exalted Him: "Therefore God has highly exalted Him and bestowed on Him the name that is above every name, so that at the name of Jesus every knee should bow, in heaven and on earth and under the earth, and every tongue confess that Jesus Christ is Lord" (Phil 2:9–11).

Do you recall the first time you discovered the meaning of your name? Perhaps you saw your name written on a coffee cup and the meaning spelled out. Or perhaps you saw your name on a wooden plaque at a gift shop, and your name took on new meaning. It may have even redirected your life as you began to try to live up to your name. Jesus knew all along the meaning of His name. And today, as we begin a new day, a new month, a new year, let us hold on anew to the meaning of the name of Jesus. It has personal meaning and significance for you. Jesus means Savior—your Savior; your Savior for today, for this year, forever.

Rev. Jerrold L. Nichols

The Baby Named Jesus

Luke 2:21–24

And they called His name Jesus, which means "Yahweh saves," because He would save His people from their sins. How He did the saving is at the heart of what happened to Jesus on the eighth day of His life, when two refugees from Galilee came to the local rabbi in Bethlehem, bearing their little baby. They came for the baby to be marked in His own flesh with the sign of God's covenant with Abraham and thus to obligate Him to keep the entire Law that God had given Moses. The summary of the Law is simply the word *love*: love for God above all things and love for the neighbor as the self. So the baby was laid down, and His foreskin was cut clean with a knife of flint. Blood was spilled—the promise of greater bloodshed yet to come.

We gather today, this first day of a new year, to celebrate with Christians across the world the circumcision and naming of a Jewish baby two millennia ago.

THE GOD WHO MAKES PROMISES

The God who has made us His own is a God who makes lavish, outrageous promises that boggle the imagination and defy reason and common sense. To Abram God made promises. Abram lived four thousand years ago in what we now call Iraq. He was 70 years old, living a settled and peaceful life—albeit a little sad. He and his wife had no children. They were rich by anyone's standards. They had all that life could bring, except a baby. This man, of all the men in the world, our God singled out and made promises: (1) You will become a great nation, with kings coming from your body; (2) You will have your own land in which to dwell; (3) Through you and your offspring blessing will come to all nations of the world. Thus went the lavish, outrageous, mind-boggling, reason-defying promises of God. Amazingly, Abraham believed those promises, even though they hinged on his having a child. Despite his advanced age and his wife who was past the years of childbearing, he trusted that if God makes a promise, God will keep it, no matter how impossible it seems.

The sign of circumcision was to be a constant reminder to God's people of what God had promised Abram: that one day the Seed would come who would bless all nations and would come out of Abraham's and Sarah's own flesh and blood.

The Law of Holiness

The same God who makes these lavish promises is also a God who is awesome and terrible in His holiness. So when He makes a people His own, His holy people, He lays down on them the Law of His holiness. To belong to Him who is burning holiness and shining love, their lives must also be burning holiness and shining love. Through Moses God gave the Law in ten clear and terrifying utterances. When the people heard God speak them, they stopped their ears and pleaded that they hear Him speak no more directly, but only through Moses. Moses, according to God's instruction, joined the sign of the promise to Abram with the obligation to keep the Law. Now, you must be perfectly clear on this: the Law of God promises everlasting life and salvation to everyone who keeps it perfectly. And it threatens judgment and eternal condemnation to everyone who breaks it, even one who breaks it only once.

His name shall be called Jesus, for He will save His people from their sins. The rabbi cut the sign of the promise and the sign of the obligation upon His infant flesh. Here is the last and great and final circumcision in the sense of the promise to Abraham, for here in the flesh of this Child we encounter the one who would come from Abraham's descent and bring blessing to all the families of the earth. This is the one to which all the circumcisions of the Jewish race are pointed. Now He lives on earth as the Promised One. But how will He bring the blessing? What will the blessing be?

The blessing He brings is that He takes the obligation of the Law upon Himself. He does what no one had ever done before. He keeps it flawlessly and perfectly. He came to live the life that we have all failed to live, the life that God's holy and unchanging Law demands must be lived if we are to have eternal life. He lived the unbroken "yes" to the Father. Never once did He draw back. Not in the Garden of Gethsemane, not on the cross, not as His body lay in the tomb. His perfect life of love never failed—the life of perfect dependence on God and the life of perfect love toward all people. Jesus lived it to the full, as He obligated Himself to do on the day of His circumcision when He was an 8-day-old infant.

Do you see, then, why we have something to celebrate on New Year's Day, why the circumcision of this baby means so much? All He took on Himself to fulfill that day He did for us, to bring the promised blessing of Abraham home to us that we might be among those who inherit the blessing of eternal life.

God is so great. He still takes little babies and puts the sign of His promise on them—but this time with water. It's the sign of His promise fulfilled, of His obligation kept. The blessing that all Jesus did for you He gives to you freely in the waters of Holy Baptism. There you receive the promised inheritance of the Holy Spirit to live in your heart as the down payment in your life that you have an eternity of joy with God. With the promise comes the obligation to live henceforth as His own, to live in love, to keep His holy commands. And here is the greatest joy: in Baptism you receive the forgiveness that Christ won for you by His life of active obedience, His perfect love—God's gift to you in the water.

When you begin each new day of this new year with the remembrance of your Baptism, do as the Catechism instructs, making the sign of the cross and saying, "In the name of the Father and of the Son and of the Holy Spirit." As you do that, each day is given you fresh and new, clean and pure as the 8-day-old Christ Child. There is no guilt for a past that is forgiven, forgotten, and lost in the sea of Baptism's grace.

We don't know what the future may bring, including this new year, but this we do know: He who has made us His own at such cost will never leave us; He will never forsake us; He will bring us home—this God of ours with His lavish and outrageous promises.

Rev. William C. Weedon

What's in a Name?

Luke 2:21

What's your name? Mine is Erwin. So what? A name is just a handle or label by which we identify each other, and it doesn't matter much whether it's Erwin or Erline, Mark or Mabel. But it wasn't always that way. Rebekah called her first son Esau because he was hairy, and that's what Esau means. She called her second son Jacob because it means "deceiver," and he would deceive his brother and take his place as firstborn.

Names meant much in those days. They either described a person's nature or character or expressed the feelings and hopes of the parents. After Rachel's sister and competitor, Leah, had ten children, Rachel called her first son Joseph, which means "may he add," because she hoped for another child. God did give her another son, whom she called Benjamin, which means "son of happiness."

My mother called me Erwin, which means "friend of the sea," but she didn't know what the name meant—it just sounded good to her. That's the way we get our names today: either we are named after another person or our parents like the sound of the name.

What's in a name? Today nothing. Anybody here named Paul? Are you small? That's what your name means. Or George? That means "one who amasses a fortune." Have you done so? Mary means "sympathetic." Philip means "lover of horses." And we could go on and on.

GOD'S NAME DESCRIBES GOD

What's in a name? Not much—except when we come to the names of God. His names reveal something about Him or His purposes. So it is with the names of Mary's Son—Jesus, Christ, and Lord. That's what we want to examine today. Today is the eighth day after our celebration of the birth of Jesus. On that day, like all good Jewish boys, Jesus was circumcised and given His name. On our calendars we call today New Year's Day, the beginning of a new year. But on the church calendar, today is called the Circumcision and Name of Jesus.

THE HISTORY OF NEW YEAR'S DAY

Picking January 1 for New Year's Day happened this way: Christmas and Easter came into the church calendar because the Church sought to counter pagan festivals. New Year celebrations came, according to Augustine, to encourage Christians to fast and pray while pagans celebrated. The Fourth Council of Toledo, AD 633, commanded fasting and abstinence on New Year's Day. Pope Boniface IX in AD 615 made it a church holiday. The first celebration was held in St. Mary's Church, the oldest church in Rome, which was dedicated to Mary. So New Year's was called the Feast of Mary. But in Gaul there was a strong emphasis on the circumcision of Jesus, and in the Middle Ages the focus turned to the name of the Lord. Later, a separate day on the calendar was given to Mary, so the Church combined circumcision and the naming of our Lord for the one day, New Year's Day. Today denominations differ in their emphasis. Roman Catholics observe the "Solemnity of Mary"; the Orthodox, the "Circumcision of Jesus Christ"; the Episcopal, the "Feast of the Holy Name." Some Lutherans focus on the name of Jesus and some on His circumcision.

THE NAME *JESUS*

What's in a name? That is the question we will ask of each name of Jesus that we examine this morning: Jesus, Christ, and Lord. First, then, the name *Jesus*.

Jesus is the English transliteration of the Greek name *Iesous*, which comes from the Hebrew *Joshua*, which means "the Lord saves." The Gospel for this day, our text, says that when Jesus was circumcised, "He was called Jesus, the name given by the angel before He was conceived" (Lk 2:21). Remember Gabriel's words to Mary: "You will conceive in your womb and bear a son, and you shall call His name Jesus" (Lk 1:31). God picked the name, and He wanted no mistake about it. In a dream the angel of the Lord said to Joseph, "She will bear a son, and you shall call His name Jesus"; and then the angel gave the reason for the name: "for He will save His people from their sins" (Mt 1:21).

One day a man picked up a good-looking stone from a mountain brook and took it home for a doorstop. After many years, a geologist visiting in the man's home was attracted to this somewhat unusual stone. After careful examination he concluded that it was gold. For years it was just an ordinary stone serving as a doorstop, but now it became famous as the biggest lump of gold ever found east of the Rockies.

Jesus came and lived as an ordinary Galilean peasant. He was known by the personal name "Jesus," and since people back then had no second or last names, He was identified by His connection to His parents, His home, or His occupation. He was Jesus, son of Joseph; Jesus, son of Mary; Jesus of Nazareth; or Jesus, the carpenter's son. But in that ordinary stone there was gold. Jesus was the promised Messiah, the Savior of the world. What's in the name *Jesus*? The Savior, who died for our sins and forgives every one of them.

Coming to the end of another year is almost like coming to the end of a life. A person who is conscious that life's end is near is always conscious of the many tasks yet undone. The British statesman and scholar Cecil Rhodes, of Rhodes scholarship fame, complained in his dying hour, "So much yet to be done." The author Helen Hunt Jackson wrote four days before her death, "I have wasted half my days. My work is only begun." Try it. Ask a person facing death if they have done everything they wanted to do. You can be pretty sure of the answer. But ask Jesus: "Did You do everything You came to do before You died?" You know the answer. He spoke it from the cross: "It is finished!"[1] All that needed to be done for our forgiveness, for our peace with God, for our eternal happiness in heaven is finished. That's what's in the name of Jesus.

THE NAME *CHRIST*

What's in the name *Christ*? Christ is not a personal name like *Jesus*, but a title of an office—like "the mayor," "the governor," "the president." Christ is the English translation of the Greek *Christos*, equivalent to the Hebrew word *Messiah*, which means "the anointed one." For four thousand years the Jews looked forward to the coming of one who would be anointed to bring God's kingdom, His rule, to earth. He would re-establish the throne of David and bring peace and justice. That's why the shepherds were so excited. The angels said this baby in the manger was "Christ the Lord" (Lk 2:11). Simeon had been told by the Holy Spirit that he would not die until he had seen "the Lord's Christ" (Lk 2:26). When the Magi came to King Herod, he asked his scholars to find out from Scripture "where the Christ was to be born" (Mt 2:4). When Jesus asked His disciples who they thought He was, Peter confessed, "You are the Christ, the Son of the living God" (Mt 16:16). Caiaphas, the high priest in Jesus' trial before the Sanhedrin, said to Jesus, "I adjure You by the living God, tell us if You are the Christ, the Son of God" (Mt 26:63). Jesus responded, "You have said so" (Mt 26:64). After the resurrection, the name of His office, Christ, came to be connected to the personal name Jesus, as we often use it today: Jesus Christ, Christ Jesus—or as Paul often used it, "our Lord Jesus Christ."

What's in a name? What's in the name *Christ*? He is our Messiah, the one anointed to be our mediator before the almighty God. He is our Prophet, Priest, and King. What's in the name *Christ*? Our name, the name *Christian*. *Christian* means a little imitation or model of Christ. Jesus Christ not only brings us peace with God, He changes our lives so that we can learn to love and forgive, to be kind and gracious as He was. That's what's in the name *Christ*.

---

1 Gerhard Aho, *The Lively Skeleton* (St. Louis: Concordia, 1977), 40.

THE NAME *LORD*

What's in the name *Lord*? The word *Lord* was used in the Greek culture in New Testament times to refer to anyone who owned property or slaves. It was a term of respect toward superiors—something like "sir." At first, this is the way it was used toward Jesus. But when someone came to believe that Jesus was the Christ, the Messiah, they called Jesus "Lord" in the way the Old Testament used the word *Lord*. There it means the almighty God. That's the way the angel of the Lord, speaking to the shepherds, referred to Jesus when he said, "Christ the Lord" (Lk 2:11). When the fisherman Peter, on the shores of the sea of Galilee, realized who Jesus was, he fell on his knees and said, "Depart from me, for I am a sinful man, O Lord" (Lk 5:8).

Jesus used the title *Lord* to refer to Himself as God. For instance, He referred to Himself as "Lord of the Sabbath" (Mt 12:8). Also, when He sent two disciples to bring the Palm Sunday donkey, He suggested they tell the owner, "The Lord needs them" (Mt 21:3). In the Upper Room, after Jesus washed the disciples' feet and before He instituted the Lord's Supper, He said, "You call Me Teacher and Lord, and you are right, for so I am" (Jn 13:13). And you remember doubting Thomas. When he recognized the risen Jesus, he confessed, "My Lord and my God!" (Jn 20:28).

In the story of the development of the Early Church (which we have in the Book of Acts), we see the use of the name *Lord* change as did the title *Christ*. It came to be used as a personal name, but always a name filled with respect and the confession that He was Master and Ruler. In this way it become the dominant method of confessing one's faith: "Jesus is Lord." Under Roman rule it became a badge of loyalty to say, "Caesar is Lord." At one time people even threw a pinch of salt to the gods while saying, "Caesar is Lord." But Christians refused both the offering to the gods and the expression. Instead they said, "Jesus is Lord." And because of it, they suffered severe persecution. But Paul assured them that one day "every tongue [would] confess that Jesus Christ is Lord" (Phil 2:11).

What's in the name *Lord*? It means that Jesus Christ is the lord of my life, the master of my destiny, the ruler of my world. He is "King of kings and Lord of lords" (1 Tim 6:15). What's in a name? Jesus—my Savior from sin; Christ—my Prophet and Priest; Lord—my King and my God.

There are other names of Jesus that are worth studying. Someone listed sixty-seven of them in the New Testament. And we could ask "What's in a name" of each of them. But as we remember His names and find hope in them, we also remember our names. God does.

In 1945 a deaf, blind teenager was found wandering the streets of Jacksonville, Illinois. He was also severely mentally challenged. Since no relatives could be located, he was placed in a state institution as John Doe No. 24. He spent the rest of his life there and died at what they guessed was age 64 from a stroke. The Associated Press told the story under the heading "John Doe 24 Takes His Secret to the Grave." At a brief graveside ceremony, a woman asked if anyone had any words to say. No one did. No one knew his name.[2]

God knows my name and He knows your name, whatever it is—Erwin or Erline, Mark or Marjorie, Mary or Paul, Jennifer or George. He sent His Son, Jesus Christ, to be our Lord, to die for us, and to gather us into His kingdom, His flock. There, Jesus promised, "He calls His own sheep by name and leads them" (Jn 10:3). Every time you hear the name Jesus—Christ—Lord, remember who He is and who you are.

Rev. Erwin J. Kolb

---

2   Max Lucado, *A Gentle Thunder* (Nashville: Word, 1995), 76–77.

Blessed Be the Name

Numbers 6:22–27

The pain of not being claimed. *(Share an experience where two captains were to choose up sides for a game and it came down to two people—you and someone else. Your heart sank when the captain picked the other person. In effect you were really never chosen; you were just assigned to one team.)*

The Israelites had been blessed by God when He freed them from slavery in Egypt. Despite that fact, they horrendously failed God as they stood at the base of Mount Sinai. They influenced Aaron to build a golden calf when Moses failed to return. In addition to worshiping idols, they engaged in immoral behavior. They also grumbled daily about their conditions in the wilderness, sounding more like children than adults, complaining about the bad food and how unfair their situation was. When God disciplined them for this unfaithfulness, many of them realized how much they had failed God. They begged for mercy (Ex 33:4–6).

We, like the Israelites, have so many blessings that we take for granted, yet we continually fail. It is January 1, and we can all look at the past year and name specific instances where we have failed God. *(Perhaps you can mention an instance where you failed God.)*

Such an evaluation is healthy when it moves us to see that sin separates us from God and then moves us to beg for mercy. Such an evaluation can move some to hopelessness. Some feel that no matter how hard they try, they fail. They feel cut off from God. This attitude, when we are stuck in it, is harmful. For those who feel this way, God offers mercy and invites us to trust His promise.

God placed His name on each Israelite with His blessing, even though they had failed Him. Just after the golden calf incident, God instructed Moses to tell Aaron to place His name on the people. The people eventually cherished God's claim on their lives.

This blessing was used extensively in their worship when people recalled God's claim on them. This blessing became significant for the Israelites at the critical moment of death. In 1986, two thin amulets were discovered in a burial cave in the Valley of Hinnom. These amulets were dated as coming from the ninth century BC. Written on the amulets was the Aaronic benediction (see Numbers

6:23–26). The people saw that by placing His name on His people at the time of their death, God claimed them for Himself.[3]

This benediction poetically cascades from three to five to seven Hebrew words, showing how God's blessings increase until they reach the number of completion. As God claimed the Israelites for Himself, He gave them all the blessings that He knew they needed.

God made a claim on His Son when He named Him *Jesus*, the one who saves. His entire ministry revolved around the salvation of a sinful world.

God places His name on each of us in Baptism. In the Great Commission of Matthew 28, where the Church is commanded to baptize, Jesus states that Baptism is to be in the (one) name of the triune God: Father, Son, and Holy Spirit. Through Baptism, we are drawn into the abundant, eternal life of the triune God. This washing away of sins and bestowal of new life is valid and powerful because it is based on the crucifixion and resurrection of Jesus Christ, an event that has already happened. *(This could be the place to mention how Martin Luther incorporated this benediction into his liturgies for Holy Communion as a change from what the rest of Christendom did. This conclusion to worship helps people leave in the assurance that God has a claim on them.)*

Although the people of Israel continued to grumble, they did survive the wilderness and enter the Promised Land.

Although we continue to sin, we can live with confidence because God has claimed us, placing His name on us. *(The best illustrations to use here are ones each preacher knows personally. One historical example is that of Bob Richards, an Olympic pole vaulter who was told he was too small for football but through the confidence the Lord gave him was able to achieve his goal. Another is the story of Eric Liddell, whose achievements as a sprinter became well–known through the movie* Chariots of Fire. *Eric Liddell went on to do missionary work in China. Shortly before his death, he went out while fighting was being waged all around to bring in two wounded men to a hospital. He was eventually captured by the Japanese and died in a prison camp. He truly knew God's claim on him.)*

(At this point the preacher could share a particular challenge that he sees for his congregation in the year ahead. He might encourage them, in God's name and strength, to strive to reach their goal.)

Many Christian schools begin the academic year by singing "With the Lord Begin Your Task." Listen to the words:

---

3   Baruch A. Levine, *Numbers 1–20*, Anchor Bible Commentary (New York: Doubleday, 1993), 238–41. These amulets omitted the two sequential phrases "and be gracious to you; the Lord turn His face toward you," perhaps because they were somewhat repetitive and also because there wasn't room for the entire benediction.

With the Lord begin your task;
Jesus will direct it.
For His aid and counsel ask;
Jesus will perfect it.
Ev'ry morn with Jesus rise,
And when day is ended,
In His name then close your eyes;
Be to Him commended. (*LSB* 869:1)

Our year begins and ends in Jesus' name. His presence and blessing will guide us through every challenge. Claimed by His grace, we are blessed in His name.

Rev. W. Philip Bruening

St. Timothy, Pastor and Confessor

Under a Shepherd's Care

John 21:15–17

Near Bordertown, South Australia, an American had the pleasure of a stay at the Graham and Gwen Koch sheep ranch. The highlight was hopping onto the back of the "ute" (short for utility pickup truck) and heading out to the four thousand acres of pasture to feed the several thousand animals. As the truck slowly approached the pasture, the animals became skittish and began to run away. Soon, however, the animals realized why the truck had come. As the feed was dispensed from the vehicle, a thousand bleating sheep clambered to receive their share. How comforted they were, sure of receiving good things, to be free to eat and be satisfied.

You and I are under a shepherd's care too. This day in the Church Year we have opportunity to consider what it is to have Christ as our Good Shepherd—to be under a shepherd's care—especially as this relates to Christ's gift of pastors or under-shepherds to His Church. What comfort, what surety and freedom are ours under a shepherd's care!

Under a shepherd's care there is comfort! What comfort to know Christ is so long-suffering with His sheep! Peter boasted of his faithfulness yet failed miserably and repeatedly (Mt 26:33). Peter's failure was followed by Christ's forgiving restoration. What comfort for us to see that Christ is such a forgiving, restoring Shepherd! How we fail miserably and repeatedly!

Under a shepherd's care, there is surety! God in Christ has determined that the forgiveness and restoration once offered Peter then and there comes to us here and now. Thus we receive the Word of forgiveness in preaching and Absolution, Holy Baptism, and the Holy Supper.

The festival of St. Timothy and its Gospel regarding the apostle Peter show us that the chief Shepherd, Jesus, uses the office and work of pastors to feed His sheep with forgiveness, life, and salvation. Preaching, Absolution, Baptism, and the Lord's Supper come to us in the concrete ministry of a real person called by the Church to stand humbly in Christ's stead, speaking Christ's words and doing Christ's deeds.

We see in the failings and humanness of two great under-shepherds—Peter, with his impetuous spirit and denials, and Timothy, with his youthful timidity and illness—that confidence in God's grace must not be based on any man, including the pastor. Like other Christians, they are sinners. (So Jesus calls Peter "Son of Jonah" to remind him of this fact.)

Nevertheless, Christ has called the under-shepherd. So sure is the calling that Luther points out that the Holy Spirit may leave the man, but not the Office of the Ministry. A pastor may undergo severe moral failure, yet the pastoral acts hold good. Why? Their power rests in Christ's office and work, not in the man.

Under a shepherd's care there is freedom! There is freedom to recognize our failings and to be forgiven by Christ. There is freedom to know that forgiveness is found in the objective merits of Christ delivered through another Christian and especially through a congregation's pastor. There is freedom to serve Christ in our respective vocations, assured of Christ's forgiveness and restoration. There is freedom to forgive others as we have been forgiven!

This sermon opened by recounting an incident that occurred on the Koch sheep ranch in Australia. The truck with visitors approached the grazing sheep. The sheep began to flee but then turned and crowded about the vehicle dispensing the food. But I omitted one thing. The animals fled until—in a voice barely audible—Graham began repeating, "Hey bob! Hey bob!" calmly speaking to the sheep. At that voice the sheep turned. In minutes the truck was engulfed in a veritable sea of sheep. They knew the shepherd's voice and that he had come to feed them. You are under the chief Shepherd's care. You know His voice and you follow Him. You also know the voice of Christ's under-shepherd, your pastor. You hear his voice as he goes about fulfilling his call—feeding, leading, protecting, and keeping this flock. By God's grace you are under a shepherd's care. In that may we all find comfort, surety, and freedom!

Rev. Matthew C. Harrison

St. Titus, Pastor and Confessor

Grasping the Love of Christ

Ephesians 3:14–21

This morning we remember how we are grasped by the love of God in Jesus Christ. It is a love that changes us. In turn, as we grasp that love, it molds and shapes us as a potter molds his clay. That love shapes us to be the work of God's hand. We grasp the love of Christ because we have been joyously grasped by it.

The Grasp of God's Love

St. Titus, whose special day we celebrate today, knew something about that divine grasp of love and grace. St. Titus was so grasped by the Gospel through the missionary work of St. Paul. Titus was a Gentile. He was a beloved companion to the apostle. Titus played a key role in the early Christian Church. He was the living object lesson of what it means to be grasped by the love of Christ. Titus went with Paul and Barnabas to Jerusalem, but Paul refused to circumcise Titus because the Gospel that grasps and its meaning for all people were on the line (Gal 2:1–10).

"You are all one in Christ Jesus" (Gal 3:28). When God justifies you in God's sight through the merits of Jesus Christ alone by your faith alone, you are free from the good work of circumcision. It's God's grasp of love that saves you. Titus provided the Jerusalem church, which was debating circumcision of the Gentiles, with the object lesson of what God's loving grasp means for anybody and everybody. Christ alone is now our justification in the sight of God! And Paul wouldn't yield one inch on that precious message of God's grasp of love in Jesus Christ of Jew and Gentile alike.

The Church's Defining Mission

That message is the Church's defining mission: to embrace a fallen world with God's grasp of love in Jesus Christ.

That is the message we proclaim to a sinful and hurting world. That is the message that shapes our grasp of others in love. God in Christ grasped you in suffering love. Now grasp others in love in the name of Christ. Be grounded in God's love in Jesus Christ. Grow in that love. Keep your eyes focused on the cross of Jesus Christ, where that love is embodied. Die with Him and rise with Him to a new life of love.

How that message must have changed Titus, a Gentile! As a Gentile, he was outside the family of God. He was excluded from being a child of God. Then he heard the message through the work of St. Paul. Titus could also belong—through Jesus Christ!

A message like that can change you. And it does! God reaches down and grasps you in His love and says, "You belong to Me now through My Son, your Savior!"

Trust the Message

Our problem, always, is not to trust the message. It shows up in the life of the Church in complaining and backbiting and apathy about mission; in ways that are not God's ways for our lives; in the emptiness of our love; in ways when we behave in a manner that doesn't reveal the love divine that has grasped us, seized us, and tries to shape us to look like Jesus, God's Son.

A lack of trust in the message has been a problem for a long, long time. Titus knew it when the Jerusalem church disagreed about circumcision. Some people in that congregation were suspicious of St. Paul and his Gospel. They didn't think Paul should so freely welcome Gentiles to the family of God. They didn't think that God's grasp of the world in love should be as grand and broad and big as it was and is.

St. Paul, however, wouldn't hear of it. He would not compromise the Gospel of God's justifying love under any circumstances! Justification is by God's grace alone through faith alone in Christ alone, apart from the works of the Law. You don't budge on a Gospel that big and strong and wonderful! Paul showed Titus how to be strong in the Lord because of a Gospel that had also grasped the Gentiles in love.

No doubt it was a great lesson for young Pastor Titus to learn from St. Paul, his teacher, mentor, and friend. It continues to be a great lesson for us today—we pastors, we people. We can't fudge on the Gospel! We can't steal people's Christian freedom. We can't rob God of His generosity, grace, goodness, and love.

Be Filled with the Fullness of God

The Ephesians text sings of that love over and over again. It is the Epistle for both the day of St. Titus and of St. Timothy, two young pastors of the early Christian Church. You can almost hear St. Paul commending such love to Titus and Timothy:

> I bow my knees before the Father . . . that according to the riches of His glory He may grant you to be strengthened with power through His Spirit in your inner being, so that Christ may dwell in your hearts through faith—that you,

being rooted and grounded in love, may have strength to comprehend with all the saints what is the breadth and length and height and depth, and to know the love of Christ that surpasses knowledge, that you may be filled with all the fullness of God. (Eph 3:14, 16–19)

What words! They are meant for us too. And how can we "be filled with all the fullness of God"? By trusting those words with the faith God has given each of us. By trusting the God whose grasp is so big and strong and powerful and deep that it cut through our sin and alienation from God with a cross. Christ Jesus bore that sin and alienation in Himself for us. Christ Jesus brings the divine life to us as His gift of grace.

Through the power of the Spirit, let that life live in you. Make your life baptismal. Die with Christ to what is old. Rise with Christ to His newness of life. Trust the power of the Gospel to remake you into God's newness.

Young Pastor Titus did. A Pharisee named Paul of Tarsus did. All the saints of heaven who have gone before us did. They trusted that Gospel. God's promise to you and to me is that the same thing can happen for each of us: to grasp Christ's love, even as we have been grasped by it forever.

Rev. Stephen C. Krueger

June

I Will Speak Your Decrees before Kings—and Anyone Else Who Will Listen

Psalm 119:43–46

"I will also speak of Your testimonies before kings and shall not be put to shame" (Ps 119:46). Martin Luther turned the words of the psalmist into a triumphal shout of praise as he heard the reports from the Diet of Augsburg at the end of June, 1530.

As an outlaw, condemned to death as a heretic and criminal by the Edict of Worms nine years earlier, Luther had not been able to accompany his followers and friends to the city of Augsburg in May 1530. There the German emperor, Charles V, was presiding over the legislature of his German lands. He had demanded that the Lutheran princes and municipal governments in his lands explain why they should not obey the law he had passed in Worms. Complying with the emperor's desire to suppress the Lutherans' confession of the faith would have had devastating consequences for that faith. It would have meant that they would sacrifice their desire to reform the Church along lines set forth by Luther.

They would have to stop proclaiming the Word of God as they had come to understand it from Luther. They would have to return to the old way of Christian living, which had directed medieval Europeans to their own activities as the insurance of their salvation.

That was not an option for these early followers of Luther. They knew that God's Word freed them from sin, guilt, fear, and death; it set them on the path of true life. They wanted their faith to flow into public confession of its saving message. They knew that people were longing to receive the gift of life that the message of Jesus Christ brings. Like Luther nine years earlier at Worms, they believed they could do nothing else but tell the Good News of life in Christ's name.

Instead of conceding and abandoning their faith, Luther's followers—led by his colleague from the University of Wittenberg, Philip Melanchthon—composed at Augsburg a confession of the faith. The Lutheran princes and municipal representatives presented it to Charles V, boldly proclaiming their message and confessing their faith. The emperor did not accept this confession. He continued to regard them as outlaws and threatened to suppress their proclamation of the Gospel by force of arms.

And the princes were prepared to sacrifice their lands and their lives for the faith. Margrave Georg of Brandenburg knelt in obedience before Charles V and offered to give up his head—to be executed—because he would not renounce his faith in Jesus Christ, as Luther had taught him to confess it. The emperor could only stumble out, "Head not off, head not off," when confronted with the margrave's bold confession of his faith.

Charles V was not so kind a quarter century later when he finally marshaled a military force to defeat the Lutheran princes on the battlefield. At that point he condemned Philip of Hesse and John Frederick of Saxony to life imprisonment for their continued confession of this faith of Augsburg. They went to prison for their faith. In the case of John Frederick, jail damaged his health so much that he died shortly after his release. His witness to the faith led to martyrdom.

Such bold conviction and fearless spirit thrilled Luther as he used the words of the psalmist to describe what was happening in his own day. The theologians and the government officials who wrote and made the confession at Augsburg refused to let the Word of God's truth be taken out of their mouths. They recognized that in this Word of truth is the hope of the world. That Word, as they had learned it from Luther, set them free from fears for their bodily welfare. The Word they confessed liberated them from earthly anxieties, even anxiety over death. It loosed their tongues to sing and proclaim God's Good News. Nothing took the Good News out of their mouths.

The spirit over which Luther exulted exhibited itself in the document we call the Augsburg Confession, composed by Melanchthon and presented to the emperor and their fellow princes by these Lutheran leaders. This spirit moved them to a series of acts of confession during the assembly at Augsburg in 1530. It is a spirit, given by the Holy Spirit, which should move Lutherans—and all Christians—to confess the faith in Jesus Christ as the Augsburg confessors did more than four and a half centuries ago.

First, this spirit rests upon and rises out of the Evangel, the Gospel, the Good News of Jesus Christ. The princes and their theologians came to Augsburg simply to confess Jesus Christ. From Luther's words they had gained the perspective of the apostles and the ancient Church. Only in Jesus Christ can fallen sinners find peace. Only in Him can they stand before God with clean hearts and clear consciences. Only in Him can their humanity be restored to its God-intended fullness once again. Only in Him are their minds renewed so that they may proceed in faith to live out the love He created us to live in.

These leading Lutherans came as sinners. One prince drank too much. Another had a tendency toward sexual sins. They all undoubtedly abused their power as princes far too often; such is the nature of temporal power in the hands of fallen humankind. They were plagued by doubts and weakness of faith; they did not understand the Gospel as well as their theologians wrote it out for them to confess. The struggle between fear and faith within their hearts must have been so fierce that they might have thought it would tear them apart. They earned no points in God's sight, or in their own, for the boldness of their confession. They came as bedraggled, beleaguered, fragile, and frustrated people. Despite their fine clothing and their troops of servants and the swords at their belts, they shared the conviction that Luther would utter on his deathbed, "We are beggars all."

For that reason they came to confess—to confess Jesus Christ as their Lord. Luther's catechisms, written the previous year, had placed that conviction in their mouths too: "I believe in Jesus Christ, my Lord." They recognized Him as the Lord who came as God in human flesh, the Creator of the universe, lying in diapers in a manger. They confessed Him as the Lord who ruled with a crown of thorns from the throne of the cross. They trusted in Him as the God who laid out His own flesh and blood to conquer death for them, who died to reclaim life for them.

The confessors at Augsburg wanted to shout His name before kings and the whole world because they knew that He was present with them. The spirit of Augsburg was also eschatological. It senses that we stand directly in the presence of God, even as we will on the Last Day. We are accountable to Him, and He stands on our side against all evil. He remains always ready to give again the gift of life with Him whenever it becomes tattered and torn—physically, emotionally, spiritually. The princes and the theologians at Augsburg acknowledged that God was present in His Word, which they proclaimed; and that Word took shape in their confession, in their telling His story, in their own Baptism, in the absolution they received, and in His body and blood in the Lord's Supper.

With that sense of Christ's presence, and with a sense that He would return soon to complete His liberation of His people from sin and death, these confessors felt themselves freed to speak fearlessly and boldly of the Savior whom they loved. Whether the world is about to end, we cannot know. But we can see God's judgment falling on this society, and so we feel a sense of urgency imposed by the hurts of people outside the Church's door. The love of Christ compels us to reach out and bring them into the true life He gives.

The princes came to Augsburg to share with other Christians their joy over life in Christ. Thus their spirit was ecumenical. They shared their convictions regarding the Gospel first with other Christians. They did not circle the wagons to protect the Word of God. They had boundless confidence in its power to do its work of killing and making alive. They were convinced that God had led them into an especially good and helpful understanding of how the Word works to bring life to sinners. They wanted fellow Christians who disagreed with them to understand what their disagreements were all about. They sought no "victories" in arguments over their foes. They sought to share and discuss the truth of God's Word so that all could share the riches of the proper understanding of what God has said to us in the Scriptures.

The spirit of these first Lutherans at Augsburg compels those who follow in their footsteps to be evangelistic. Those confessors confessed the faith so that others might believe in Jesus and thereby have life in His name. Fundamentally, the confessors at Augsburg placed their faith before the world without fear and hesitation because they wanted others to come to a knowledge of the truth and thus enjoy the wonderful gift of life with our Creator and Father.

We, their heirs in this time of the Lord's presence and grace, cannot help but share the gift of life through the Word of the Lord as they did. For this Word is in us, and it has shaped and determined our new life in Christ.

The fact of the matter is that we are always witnessing to the faith that stands at the heart of our lives. If people know we are Christians, they will always be reading something about Christ in the way we live and speak about Him—or fail to speak about Him. If people do not know we are Christians, they will sense quickly what it is that stands at the heart of our lives. If they get the impression that it is something other than Jesus Christ, we will have witnessed to the supreme importance of whatever else that might be and thus suggested that Christ is not the source and author of life. We are always witnessing to our faith. We must simply work on improving our witness.

God's Word works on us as its confessors and witnesses, for it bestows on us the forgiveness of sins. Through His Word, Christ has rescued us from death and given Himself to us as the way—the way of truth, the way to life. He has placed His Word in our mouths and freed us, so that we might fear nothing because we know we are safe in Him. That means we are not afraid to testify to the truth in the face of those who would mock or even kill us. Trusting His presence and power, we are given boldness to confess. Thus we are freed from those fears of our own inadequacy that intimidate us. For we know we are not making ourselves look good in the Father's sight by how well we witness. We know we already look good in the Father's sight because He sees us through Christ-colored glasses. We confess our faith for the sake of the neighbor who needs to hear that those who are dead in trespasses and sins can have resurrection hope in Christ.

We may, in fact, witness more effectively to the power and love of Christ when we witness with our vulnerability showing, as did the confessors at Augsburg. Because we are acquainting others with a person, Jesus of Nazareth, rather than merely acquainting them with a bunch of Bible facts, we reveal His love when our tornness and tatteredness still show. People in the struggle against evil do not have time or trust to listen to those above the fray. They don't want an expert on religion, but an experienced fellow struggler. They want someone who is living proof of the difference Christ's forgiveness can make in situations like theirs.

Therefore, we confess the faith as heirs of those first Lutherans who were called to testify before their emperor, before their empire, to God's love in Christ Jesus. They opened the mouths into which the Lord had placed His truth, and they broadcast life and salvation to their world. God calls us to do the same today. He frees us from sin and fear and every hesitation, and He gives us the power to speak His Word before kings and all manner of people. We are confident that we shall not be put to shame, for He has set us free to witness to His Word.

Rev. Robert A. Kolb

St. Peter and St. Paul

Two Old Fools

1 Corinthians 3:16–23; Mark 8:27–35

Does it offend you that I refer to St. Peter and St. Paul as "old fools"? I know it might. They are truly heroes in the Church, heroes in our eyes. But it is a title St. Paul uses for himself in the first text for today—and I expect that after being reminded of the experience at Caesarea Philippi (when Jesus called Peter "Satan") that Peter would have claimed it also. On one hand, they might be ashamed of the title. On the other hand, they might be rightly proud—and we might be urged to join them.

PETER—A FOOL

On one hand, they might be ashamed of the title. What a fool you were, Peter. What a fool you were, Paul. A couple of "old fools." How foolish of you, Peter, to think that you knew more than Jesus about how to save the world. You affirm that Jesus is the Christ. And other Gospel accounts would expand your response, noting Jesus as the Christ, the Savior of the world. Then when Jesus begins to reveal how salvation is going to take place, you think you know better—you rebuke Jesus for saying He must be killed and then rise from the dead. You make a fool out of yourself. Jesus rebukes you, saying, "Get behind Me, Satan" (Mk 8:33). You were a fool—and you knew it. Did the disciples laugh at you?

I am always a little reluctant to jump on Peter about this point. If I had said anything, I probably would have done what Peter did—try to talk Jesus into choosing another path for the salvation of all. There are other examples of Peter's foolishness. Trying to walk on the water. And, of course, saying he would die with Christ before betraying Him and then denying Christ three times before the rooster crowed. But I always try to be careful about pointing a finger at Peter. I doubt I would have done better.

PAUL—A FOOL

Paul's record is different but hardly any better. When he was still Saul, that fine young Pharisee so zealous for the faith he had been taught by his parents and by Gamaliel, he worked faithfully to snuff out the new Christian sect—even attending the stoning of Stephen. We are tempted to say that Paul was really a fool.

He must have felt that way when he was suddenly struck down on the road to Damascus.

We also have been there, done that. We have followed the teachings of our youth and even of some teachers of our age and have come to understand that they stood in direct opposition to what God in Christ was calling us to do and to be—and we felt like such fools.

We Are Fools Too

Two old fools—and we are added to their number. Old fools who stand before God with egg on our face. Old fools who have done ourselves no credit. Old fools whose only hope is in the mercy and grace of God. Old fools who deserve to hear again and again the mocking laughter and rejection of God. Old fools who receive instead, again and again, the forgiving love and warm embrace of God. Old fools who see in the mockery that Jesus received from the soldiers and the temple guard the mockery and abuse we deserve. Old fools who see in the sacrifice of Christ on the cross, in His suffering and death, the suffering and death that we deserve.

Old fools who see in the resurrection of Christ the only hope we have for our foolish thoughts and our foolish actions. Old fools who see in the bread and wine of Holy Communion that God does not reject fools. Instead, He forgives us, renews us, empowers us, and sends us. God sends us to use our bodies, these temples of the Holy Spirit, to live in the world as fools without the world's wisdom. Old fools for Christ. That is what Paul means in 1 Corinthians—live so the world may call you an old fool, but in God's eyes your life will be full of wisdom.

The Journey of Fools

Peter lived as a fool, as you know, by taking the Gospel to the Jewish world. Beginning on Pentecost, he proclaimed Jesus Christ as Lord wherever and whenever he could. He proclaimed Jesus as the Savior. He proclaimed Jesus' suffering and death on the cross and His glorious resurrection from the grave. Peter's journey ended in Rome, according to tradition, on June 29, AD 67.

Paul lived as a fool, as you know, when the scales were removed from his eyes so he could see Jesus, his Lord and Savior. He proclaimed the Gospel of Jesus Christ to the Gentile world. We know much of his witness, of how foolish he was perceived until his journey, according to tradition, ended in Rome on June 29, AD 67.

Both of these great men, these old fools, dedicated their life, as well as their death, to Jesus. According to tradition, Peter was crucified upside down by request. He did not consider himself worthy to be crucified the same way as Jesus was. Paul was martyred in the persecution of Nero. Two old fools.

We stand in their foolishness today—persons who have made fools of ourselves in the eyes of God but who have been forgiven. Persons who are determined to use our bodies, "temples of the Holy Spirit" (see 1 Cor 6:19), as a faithful and powerful response to the love and grace of God. Some call us foolish. We are in good company. There is nothing more important than our relationship with our forgiving and empowering God, saying in our homes, in our community, and in our world that Jesus Christ is our Lord and Savior. That allows us to join the two old fools on this June 29 in proclaiming, "You are the Christ, the Son of the living God" (Mt 16:16)!

Rev. Vernon D. Gundermann

July

Mary Magdalene

Mary, Mary Quite Contrary

John 20:1–2, 11–18

The picture of Mary Magdalene crying as she stands outside the garden tomb where Jesus had been buried is easily recalled by those who live as Easter people.

But often missed are the stark contrasts that the inspiring artist, the Holy Spirit, has painted in the portrait. Our eyes are drawn to her tears, but we often miss the background. We see the woman; but often, like Mary herself, we miss the Man who stands behind her. While noting the tomb of death, we miss the tree of life that looms in the distance.

It's a fascinating portrait: Mary, Mary, quite contrary.

Mary Magdalene was a woman possessed. Possessed by what? That depends on when you meet her, for timing is everything if you want an answer to the question.

If we meet her before she met the one called Jesus, then we find a woman possessed by seven demons (Lk 8:2). But she was about to experience the miracle of life in the man from Nazareth whom they called Jesus. In a word, possibly a touch, or perhaps as He called her by name, the demons were removed and replaced with a peace that she had never known before. Mary had seen the one who was Lord even over demons, and her life would never be the same.

Her days in this new life would be a stark contrast to her former ways. Her life now had meaning and purpose. The Gospel writers tell us that Mary was traveling with Jesus along with the disciples and others who had been recipients of His miracles. She spent her days listening and learning from her Teacher, as her faith bloomed and grew through His words and life. She joined the other women who followed Jesus. He had cast demons out of some of the other women too. Together they spent their own money in providing for Him as He went from town to town, proclaiming the kingdom of God (Lk 8:1–3). This was a woman now possessed with the Spirit of the living God, a woman who had been through Satan's hell and had now been graciously handed heaven and all its riches by Jesus Christ. The Giver of those gifts gave her a life totally contrary to her former life. She gave her life to the One who gave her life.

I would imagine that the picture is starting to come to life, and you see that this is not only Mary's picture but also ours. Certainly Mary's transformation may appear at first to be a bit more dramatic than ours. If you have difficulty remembering your former life, Scripture has recorded the details for you. It paints a description of one who was an enemy of God, apart from God, blind to His way. "Quite contrary" describes not only Mary but also you and me.

The grace of God in calling us by name is no less dramatic. That happens in Holy Baptism. And the contrast is just as startling. Mary, as we noted, was possessed by seven demons. We affirm that we too were born in sin; we were members of the devil's kingdom of darkness. But in Holy Baptism we renounce the devil and all his works and all his ways. (The older Lutheran baptismal service even included the "little exorcism.") We are marked with the cross as one redeemed by Christ the crucified. We are called by name as a child of the heavenly Father. We are welcomed into the kingdom of God to work with our fellow believers, even as Mary served among Jesus' followers. The love of our saving God poured out on us in Baptism is just as intimate as the love Jesus showed to Mary. And the Gospel that changes us is the same Gospel that changed her.

Daily we join Mary and fellow miracle recipients in traveling to Calvary and to the garden tomb owned by Joseph of Arimathea. What a joy to relive the miracle and witness the love! It reminds us that in Baptism we have been crucified with Christ and raised with Him to new life. Imagine that we are there, witnessing the events as God's salvation unfolds.

On the day that Jesus was crucified, Scripture tells us that Mary stood at a distance. We can probably relate to her position, for it seems safer to hold the cross at a distance. But in doing so, we also hold our nail-scarred Savior at a distance. And we miss so much! His words of forgiveness could easily be lost amid the sound of the rumbling thunder. Even His final words of victory could by muffled by the loud sobbing and mocking jeers of the crowd.

On Easter morning the empty cross may be in the background, but don't miss the fact that it is in the center of the picture. It is what draws you into the picture and causes your eyes to be taken off Mary's tears. The cross focuses your attention on the living Man it once held in its grip.

As we approach the garden, we find Mary engrossed in her own sorrow. Her tears were real; she was grieving. But in coming so close to grieving as one who has no hope, she almost missed the miracle of life for a second time. How easy it must have been to despair at the moment. Had it all been in vain, now that Jesus was dead? And now His body seemed to be stolen. Where was the hope in going on? Perhaps she was tempted to revert to her former life. Desperate, grieving, and remembering, Mary stood in a puddle of her tears.

On that Sunday after Jesus was crucified, Mary stood outside the tomb, not in it. She had spent too much time already in a tomb of death when she was possessed by Satan and his demons. She knew she didn't want to go back into one. She had witnessed the miracle of new life once already, when Jesus brought her from death to life as He removed the demons. Did she doubt that it could happen again? She had to wonder, I would imagine, for the seemingly hopeless situation was hitting too close to home. Satan was knocking on the door again. But now she was a woman possessed by God. She had been called by name and given new life in Christ.

Now, outside the tomb, He was calling her by name again. And the miracle of life would be repeated. Contrary to standing at a distance from her Savior as He was dying on the cross, she now wanted to hold on to Him for dear life. At that particular time Jesus could not allow that physically. But by the power of God's Spirit, she held on to her Living Miracle for dear, eternal life.

The picture painted is a contrasting one. Mary's life was such. As a contrary person, Mary could see only a gardener and not the One who created the garden. Although she previously saw the messengers of God, she almost missed God Himself. As her contrary old self, she could see only hopelessness and despair, only the reasons to cry tears of sadness. But then she heard and recognized the one Lord who called her name, and she was changed. Her new life basked in the glory of a sure and certain hope through God's presence and promises. Here was the One who would eternally wipe every tear from her eyes.

These two stories are more similar than we like to admit—Mary's and ours. Once we lived in darkness amid the tears of hopelessness; but in Baptism we were buried with Christ and raised to new life. There the living Lord called us by name and said, "You are Mine forever." What a contrast to our former way of life!

Once possessed by demons, Mary knew about name-calling. But contrary to that life, she was now basking in the miracle of new life because of the one named Jesus, who called her by name and claimed her as His own child. Mary, who once was living blindly in the darkness, was now living in the light, for she had seen the Lord.

Oh, Mary, Mary, quite contrary; how your faith, as you stand in Joseph's garden, grows—for you have seen the Lord! What a portrait of a woman possessed— now possessed by the living God!

Rev. Timothy P. Wesemann

St. James the Elder, Apostle

GOD'S DEMOTION, OUR PROMOTION

Mark 10:35–45

Introduction: James, the son of Zebedee and the brother of John, is not a popular biblical hero today. Ask a hundred Christians to name the apostle most influential for their spiritual life, and few would name James. His brother, John, is certainly known better and admired more. Yet James was the first apostle to die a martyr's death, and the Church has set aside a special day, July 25, to remember his life and ministry.

Out of respect for that tradition and in the confidence that we can learn from the example of James's saintly life, the sermon focuses on the apostle James in general and on the specific incident in which he asks to share Jesus' glory. The goal is to see our own spiritual struggle mirrored in James. We, too, are self-centered and seek power and glory. More important, our goal also is to see more clearly Jesus' humiliation as the basis for saving grace to James, to us, and to all people.

1. God's Demotion.
   A. James demotes Jesus for self-promotion.
      (1) The request: a seat in glory.
      (2) *Application:* Do we use church membership to seek special favors from God or people? Do we want faithfulness to mean less personal suffering or more success? Do we contribute time, service, or money to manipulate others or to have our will done for our benefit?
   B. God is demoted when understood like human rulers.
      (1) Jesus contrasts self-promotion of worldly rulers and God's call for promotion in service. The irony of promotion in demotion.
      (2) *Application:* Absolute dictators commit obvious brutalities. From the concentration camps of World War II to the killing fields of Asia, examples abound of senseless, destructive political power. Illustrate also in less dramatic ways how ordinary, selfish human beings hurt others when they look out only for themselves.
   C. The gracious demotion of Jesus means ransomed promotion for all.
      (1) Jesus humbles Himself unto death. He will drink the cup of suffering and be buried in the baptism of death.
      (2) The death is a ransom for others. Like freeing a slave or, today, paying someone else's fine, Jesus pays the price.

2. Our promotion. The teaching and ransom-giving ministry of Jesus elevates a selfish "Son of Thunder" to sainthood. In Christ, James' life provides a model and hope for our lives.

   A. His spiritual background: one of the Twelve with special experiences.

      (1) His call (Mk 1:19–20; Mt 4:18–22). Our baptismal call to discipleship.

      (2) Present at the raising of Jairus's daughter (Mk 5:37–43). Our witness of God's life-restoring power.

      (3) Present at the transfiguration (Mk 9:2–9). Our witness of God's glory.

      (4) Present near Jesus in Gethsemane (Mk 14:33–42). Even when we are weak and weary, Jesus is praying for our salvation. He is our ransom.

   B. A special death: James was the first of the Twelve to be martyred (Acts 12:1–3a). Martyrdom means *witness*. Illustrate how Christian witness today, in life and death, gives glory to God.

Conclusion: The Tomb of the Unknowns in Arlington Cemetery in Washington, DC, inspires national patriotism. One soldier's remains have recently been identified, but others remain unknown. The lack of identity makes the sacrifice poignant and meaningful. Their anonymous but total sacrifice achieves an inspiring glory that overshadows the exploits of famous generals or admirals. How much more glorious shines the demotion of the Son of God to death on a cross, which ransomed us from lives of selfish self-promotion. Our promotion, our heavenly glory, and our lives of loving service rest on Jesus' demotion in the bitter cup and drowning baptism of death. James experienced that gracious gift, and we, learning from his wrong questions, see the glory of God.

Rev. Robert A. Holst

Lord, Not What I Want, But What I Need

Mark 10:35–45

Jesus takes the lead. He goes up the road toward Jerusalem. Our Lord's disciples are both amazed and afraid, but they tag along. Pioneer and perfecter of our faith that He is, our Lord leads the way to Jerusalem, the city of the temple, the place of sacrifice. But for the Lord Jesus, the sacrifice will take place outside the city walls, not in the temple. On the way to Jerusalem, the Lord takes the Twelve aside and discloses to them the purpose of this Passover trip: "See, we are going up to Jerusalem, and the Son of Man will be delivered over to the chief priests and the scribes, and they will condemn Him to death and deliver Him over to the Gentiles. And they will mock Him and spit on Him, and flog Him and kill Him. And after three days He will rise" (Mk 10:33–34).

This was the third time that our Lord had predicted His Passion, yet the disciples still did not understand Him. James and John came to the Lord with a prayer. Not comprehending the purpose of this journey up to Jerusalem, their prayer is off-center. In fact, it is downright selfish. "Teacher, we want You to do for us whatever we ask of You" (Mk 10:35). "Jesus, You just sign the check and we will fill in the amount!" We can well imagine the logic that transpired within the minds of Zebedee's sons. No doubt they reasoned, "We left our dad's fishing business for this life on the road. And the good Lord did promise to take care of us. So now we'll ask Him to make good that promise. He did say, 'Ask and you will receive.' Now we're asking."

If the prayer of James and John strikes you as amazing, so also is the Lord's response. He does not throw up His hands in despair over these two disciples' foolish supplication. Instead, He gently and patiently says, "What do you want Me to do for you?" (Mk 10:36). By their answer to that question, James and John demonstrate that what they want is not what they need.

James and John want glory. "Grant us to sit, one at Your right hand and one at Your left, in Your glory" (Mk 10:37). In other words, "Let one of us be president and the other vice president over the corporation of Your Church." Zebedee's sons want posts of prestige, places of high position, stations of status. But such is not what they need. What James and John need is what every disciple of Jesus Christ needs. They need, as we need, the Lord's service to us: His life-giving ransom on the cross. They need the death of the Righteous One for an unrighteous world.

We need it, too, because we are like James and John, or we are like the other ten disciples. Like James and John, we become greedy for glory in God's kingdom, almost as if God owes us something for our years of service to Him. The confident boldness that our Lord wills us to have in our praying degenerates into a bossiness before God. We become like the man praying for patience, saying, "Lord, I want patience—right now!" We treat God as though His sole reason for existence is to be a supply house for all of our desires, no matter how self-centered.

Or if we are not like James and John, we can be like the remaining ten disciples: we become envious of the gifts that the Father gives to our brothers and sisters. We complain of their unworthiness, rather than repent of our own. The Lord Jesus Christ willed to release James and John from the slavery of their greed, and the rest of His disciples from the bitterness of their envy. That release is His ransom: "The Son of Man came not to be served but to serve, and to give His life as a ransom for many" (Mk 10:45). Ransom is the price that is paid to free someone from slavery. Slaves do not earn wages; hence they cannot purchase their own freedom. The ransom must be paid by an outside party. In the language of the Old Testament, that outside party was called a *redeemer*.

Our Redeemer is Jesus Christ. He paid the price, not with silver or gold but with His holy blood, His innocent suffering and death. That blood frees us from sin, death, and hell. Our Lord's cross, freely carried for us, shapes our praying. His cross frees us to call God "our Father."

In fact, the prayer that our Lord teaches His disciples to pray is possible only because of the cross. To know the crucified Son is to know the Father. Knowing the Father through His Son, Jesus Christ, we are given the confidence and the courage to ask Him to give us not what we want but what we need, not what we want but what He wills. God wills that His name be hallowed—made holy in us as we cling to His Word with singular and undivided faith and live a holy life in accordance with that Word. God wills to give us His kingdom through faith in Christ Jesus. God wills to have His good and gracious will done in our lives; He desires that our will be brought into perfect alignment with His will. Our Father delights to give us our daily bread, for He is the Lord who opens His loving hand to satisfy the desire of every living creature. He wills that we forgive the sins of those who sin against us, just as He forgives our sins fully and freely for Jesus' sake. He wills to deliver us from every evil to body and soul and bring us at last to live with Him forever in a new creation, the home of righteousness. He wills that we receive all His great and precious gifts with the sturdy "amen" of faith. In other words, when we pray as the Lord Jesus has taught us to pray, we are asking the

Father to give us not what we want or think we want, but what we need—what He knows we need.

A man complained to the pastor that the liturgy did not say what he wanted to say. The pastor shrewdly responded that the real question is, "Are you saying what God wants you to say—what the liturgy wants you to say?" Are you confessing your sins? Are you learning to ask God for that which He promises in His Word to give you? Are you putting your "amen" to His Word and truth? Are you asking the Father to give you what you want, or what you need?

Sometimes when the Lord gives us what we need, He gives us pain. For James and John there would be a cup and a baptism. *Cup* and *baptism* indicate suffering for us, as they did for our Lord. James would taste that cup and be plunged into that baptism in Jerusalem as He became the first of the Twelve to die a martyr's death. So we sing of James the Elder today:

> O Lord, for James we praise You,
> Who fell to Herod's sword;
> He drank the cup of suff'ring
> And thus fulfilled Your word.
> Lord, curb our vain impatience
> For glory and for fame,
> Equip us for such suff'rings
> As glorify Your name. (*LSB* 518:21)

The cup and baptism of suffering are also for us—perhaps not in the form of martyrdom, but surely in the daily death to sin that God set in motion in Holy Baptism. It hurts when God divorces the sinner from his or her sin. It hurts when God nails our old, sin-infected flesh to Jesus' cross. It hurts when God does a heart transplant on us, taking from us the heart hardened and made brittle by sin and creating in us a new heart that beats by grace through faith. But that is a hurt that we can rejoice in, says the apostle Paul (Rom 5:1–5). In that tribulation, God Himself is cultivating perseverance; and through the perseverance, character; and through the character He forms hope; "and hope does not put us to shame, because God's love has been poured into our hearts through the Holy Spirit who has been given to us" (Rom 5:5).

The Lord takes away in order to give. He took away the puny little prayer of James and John to give them something far greater. James and John wanted prestige; they needed salvation. They wanted status; they needed to learn the simplicity of servanthood. The Lord gave them what they needed: His cross and empty tomb. From this Lord Jesus Christ, crucified and risen, learn to pray in faith, "Lord, give me not what I want, but what I need. Amen."

Rev. John T. Pless

August

St. Lawrence, Deacon and Martyr

Finding the Treasure

Psalm 112:1, 9

Late in His ministry, Jesus told His disciples, "If they persecuted me, they will also persecute you" (Jn 15:20). His words became painfully true for St. Lawrence. A short history lesson returns us to the third century, the last days of persecution of the early Christians by the Roman government. Lawrence was born in Spain but was led to the center of the empire at Rome and to service in the Church as a deacon.

The emperor Valerian decreed the death of all leaders of the Church at Rome, including the bishop, Pope Sixtus II, and his deacons. Lawrence, only in his 30s, was marked for an early death as a martyr. But he did not run from his responsibilities as a servant of God's people. Lawrence was the kind of person the psalmist speaks about in today's text, "Blessed is the man who fears the LORD, who greatly delights in His commandments!" (112:1). Lawrence found delight in obeying the Lord's commands and in serving His people.

Deacons in the Early Church did many of the same things that deacons do in our churches today. They care for the social and physical needs of the people. In Lawrence's time, the churches in Rome cared for the physical needs of more than 1,500 poor people. They even sent contributions to meet the needs of the poor in other parts of the empire.

Christian charity is an indication of God's people at work in all generations. As we listen to Lawrence's story, we might ask ourselves how we treasure the opportunity to be servants in Jesus' name. Is our service only occasional and halfhearted? Are we willing to give our all for others? Lawrence did. He had a gift for giving and sharing, which got him into difficulty.

Great cities and nations were just as short of cash in the third century as they are in the twenty-first century. As the local prefect looked for new revenue sources for Rome, he cast an envious eye on the money Lawrence was sending to Christians in other lands. He demanded that Lawrence bring him all the wealth of the Church. The prefect gave him three days to complete the task. Talk about stress!

But Lawrence was not without a sense of humor—a good thing for God's people to have. According to tradition, three days later, Lawrence came to the prefect—but not with silver or gold. He brought people. He brought thousands of people—poor people, blind and sick people, widows, and elderly people. Surrounded by people, he stood before the prefect and exclaimed, "The Church is truly rich, far richer than your emperor. These are her riches." Lawrence knew that people—living souls redeemed by Jesus Christ—are of far greater value than things. They are valuable because Christ has made them valuable. They are valuable because they have laid hold of the greatest treasure of all—the holy precious blood and the innocent suffering and death of Jesus Christ.

That is the way God sees it and so do His faithful and loving servants. By God's grace we have received what St. Paul calls "the unsearchable riches of Christ" (Eph 3:8). We know the life-changing Gospel of the forgiveness of sins through the suffering, death, and resurrection of Jesus Christ, our Lord. That Gospel does more than enrich our lives. It also enables us to respond with God's love to enrich the lives of others as we reach out to all people, including the poor, the sick, and the hungry.

Centuries before the time of Lawrence, the psalmist noted in today's text that sharing resources with the poor is one of the hallmarks of people who live according to God's commands. He said that the man who follows the Lord and finds delight in His commands "has distributed freely; he has given to the poor" (11:9). As we look at our incomes and our "outgos," we might reflect on how we do, or do not, scatter abroad our gifts to the poor. Blessings many times over are found in generosity (Deut 15:10; Prov 22:9; Lk 6:38). Through the ages the life of St. Lawrence has stood as a powerful example of God's grace. Although the spelling and pronunciation of his name may vary from place to place (St. Laurence in France and Canada, St. Lorenz in Germany and Michigan), the story of this third-century saint is well-known and his memory is blessed among us.

The account of St. Lawrence's earthly life ends abruptly. He died as a martyr almost immediately after presenting the "treasure of people" to the Roman official. The prefect was so enraged by his presentation of the "true riches of the Church" that he ordered a slow death by fire for the young deacon. Even then, Lawrence did not lose his sense of humor. Tradition says that as he was being grilled over the fire, he asked the executioner to turn him over as he was "broiled enough on one side."

Before he died, Lawrence prayed for the conversion of Rome. God answered his prayer. The city became Christian over the next decades and the persecutions ended. Lawrence kept the faith as a witness and a martyr. His faithful living and dying influenced many Christians of later eras. Martin Luther frequently referred to Lawrence in his lectures, noting how in Christ he "overcame death and all tortures." In an extended commentary on Ps 116:5, Luther specifically speaks of St. Lawrence and writes, "We should not abhor the cup or belittle God's gifts or be ungrateful in sufferings, because this cup is salutary, because 'precious in the sight of the Lord is the death of His saints' " (AE 11:405). Lawrence's faithfulness unto death, his care for the poor, and his generosity are parts of the example he leaves for us as we observe his day so many years after his martyrdom.

Rev. Gregory Just Wismar

St. Mary, Mother of Our Lord

M Is for Mary—and More!

Luke 1:38

The largest Christian church in the Holy Land is not located in Jerusalem or Beth-lehem. Rather, it is the Basilica of the Annunciation, sixty-five miles north of Jerusalem in Nazareth in the Galilee region. This massive and beautiful church, built in the 1960s, is constructed over the traditional site of Mary's childhood home, where the annunciation would have taken place. One of the design features of the church is the use of the letter *M* in the construction. Local guides in the church tell pilgrims that the *M* is for Mary—and much more. *M* is for *mystery*, *mother*, and *magnify*. *Magnify* is the key word in the marvelous song of Mary, called the Magnificat, which is the Gospel for today. The Christian Church has set aside August 15 as a special day to thank God for Mary and to remember, appreci-ate, and learn from the example she set for us. May her attitude of service be ours: "I am the servant of the Lord; let it be to me according to Your word" (Lk 1:38).

M Is for Mystery

There is much mystery about Mary. The Gospel writers do not tell us much about her. We do not know if she was short or tall, had dark or light hair, or what her family life was like when she was growing up. Reliable tradition portrays her as a young girl who attended her daily duties in the little village of Nazareth. This would include tasks such as baking bread and carrying water from the town well to her home. We do know a little of her family history. She could trace her heritage back to David, one of Israel's greatest kings. By the time of Mary's life, hard times had come to that royal family. The tree of the line of David had been reduced to little more than a stump. Other families had taken leadership among God's chosen people.

It seemed as though God's promises, that the Messiah would come from the family of David, could not possibly find fulfillment. But God remembers His promises. In His mysterious way, at the right time, He chose Mary to be the mother of Jesus, the Christ. It is a mysterious choice, but a blessed one. Martin Luther writes: "But when all seemed most unlikely—comes Christ, and is born of the despised stump, of the poor and lowly maiden! The rod and flower springs from her whom Sir Annas' or Caiaphas' daughter would not have deigned to have for her humblest lady's maid. Thus God's work and His eyes are in the depths, but man's only in the height" (AE 21:302). God's surprising announcement, brought by the angel Gabriel, came to Mary, an ordinary girl in a tiny, hill country village. And though she was amazed by the angel's word, without hesitation she agreed to fulfill the role of servant that has distinguished her for all generations.

In that willingness to serve God, Mary is an example to all Christians. Her obedience to God's calling at times brought her great sorrow and loneliness, but she accepted that as part of the service she was called upon to perform. Sometimes a task to which God calls us, though not as momentous as that of Mary's, may bring us disappointment and frustration. Still, we are called to echo her simple words of willing obedience and devotion: "I am the servant of the Lord." It is a great blessing to serve the Lord. As Mary herself said, "For behold, from now on all generations will call me blessed; for He who is mighty has done great things for me" (vv. 48–49). In calling Mary "blessed," we are not unduly elevating her beyond her humanity. Instead, we are honoring God for the grace He bestowed upon her in choosing her to be the virgin mother of our Savior.

M Is for Mother

Mothers have a strong formative influence with most children. That certainly was the case in the home in Nazareth when Jesus was growing up. The role of the mother in Jesus' day was clearly defined. Her responsibilities centered in domestic jobs and in meeting the needs of her family. Her personal piety would influence the religious atmosphere in her home. Mary's personal devotion to God was seen by Jesus in the early years of His childhood. In the one biblical account we have of Jesus as an adolescent, we read that the entire family made the trip from Nazareth to Jerusalem to worship at the temple each year (Lk 2:41). As He grew up, Jesus no doubt was very familiar with the local synagogue to which He returned to preach when He began His ministry (Lk 4:14–30).

He was well acquainted with the sacred things in life. Mary made sure of it. She took the time needed, for she had her priorities straight. In our technological age of e-mail and Web sites and overwhelming personal schedules, we might look back to the time of Mary and say to ourselves that life was simpler then; people had all the time in the world; they could devote more of each day or each week to their faith. But that really is not the case. Life was much harder and shorter then. Just getting enough to eat for a day was often a challenge. The day-to-day business of life filled up each daylight hour—and only the daylight hours could really be productive. Mary and Joseph made time for faith in their home. Jesus learned His religious lessons so well that the temple teachers in Jerusalem were astonished by what the young boy from the countryside of Galilee knew. He had been well instructed. That instruction began at home with Mary, His mother.

Perhaps it is helpful that Mary's day on the calendar comes as the summertime eases into the school year. We are starting to think of education once again. It is time to learn. But what kind of learning is really the most important? Mary knew. She knew the things of God well. When Gabriel told her that the Holy One to be born of her would be called the Son of God, Mary knew that the ancient messianic prophecies were about to be fulfilled (Lk 1:54–55). She didn't fully understand all that was involved in the work the Messiah was to do—to suffer and die for the sins of the world on the horrible cross—but she was willing to accept whatever God wanted her to do. The weeks ahead will bring us opportunities to grow in our understanding of God's plan of salvation and in living our faith in a way that reflects the blessed model Mary established—the caring mother who could respond firmly to the angel of the Lord with the agreeing words: "Let it be to me according to your word" (Lk 1:38). Mary's faith was simply spoken. She would be the virgin mother according to God's plan. "And the angel departed from her," writes St. Luke. Gabriel knew that Jesus would be in good and loving hands.

M Is for Magnify

In Mary's song, she uses words of praise not for herself but for God. "My soul magnifies the Lord," she sings, "and my spirit rejoices in God my Savior" (vv. 46–47). As the Lutheran Confessions relate: "Although she is most worthy of the most plentiful honors, yet she does not want to be made equal to Christ. Instead she wants us to consider and follow her example" (Apology of the Augsburg Confession XXI 27; *Concordia*, p. 205). Throughout her life, Mary defers to her Son, Jesus, her Savior and ours. She brings her concerns to Him at the wedding at Cana and at other times. She puts the care of her life in His hands, accepting His provision for her in His word from the cross. And, as we see her for the final time in the Book of Acts, she joins the disciples and the women in the Upper Room in bringing her prayers to the ascended Lord. Mary had come to understand that it was through her Son's suffering and death for the sins of all people that God's promised salvation is found. And Mary knew the proper life-long response of being redeemed by God: she magnifies the Lord. Her words run over with a beauty and a fullness of faith that comes down through the centuries to us: "He who is mighty has done great things for me, and holy is His name" (Lk 1:49). Our mighty and loving God has done great things for us all, just as He did for the young girl from Nazareth.

M is for Mary—and much more. As we take the special opportunity this day affords us in the life of the Church, we can bless God for the virgin mother of our Lord Jesus. Through Him the gracious and mysterious plan of salvation was accomplished. Remembering God's goodness and mercy, we join in magnifying His holy name, joyfully singing with Mary, "My soul magnifies the Lord" (v. 46)!

Rev. Gregory Just Wismar

St. Bartholomew, Apostle

From Skeptic to Apostle

John 1:43–51

The history of God's holy Church is replete with men and women who, by the Spirit's working in the Gospel, have been brought from unbelief and skepticism to a lively faith in the Son of God. In our own day, we think of C. S. Lewis, an English intellectual who tells of his conversion from atheism to Christianity in his autobiography, *Surprised by Joy*, or the British journalist Malcolm Muggeridge, whose skepticism is dispelled by Him who is the way, the truth, and the life. Today the Church celebrates the day of St. Bartholomew, apostle. Bartholomew (or Nathanael, as he is named in St. John's Gospel) is delivered from skepticism to faith in Jesus, the King of Israel.

It all happens just after our Lord's Baptism in the river Jordan. John the Baptist acclaims the freshly baptized Lord as "the Lamb of God" (v. 36). Andrew and Simon Peter follow the Lamb. From the Jordan, Jesus moves toward Galilee. There He finds Philip and calls Him to discipleship. The Word of the Lord moves from ear to heart to tongue and into the ear of Bartholomew as Philip says to him, "We have found Him of whom Moses in the Law and also the prophets wrote, Jesus of Nazareth" (Jn 1:45).

The Lord uses the simplicity of Philip's confession to bring Bartholomew from skepticism to salvation. Luther writes of this miracle:

He [Jesus] studiously avoided the city of Jerusalem with its royal throne, the residence of the mightiest, richest, and wisest. He refrained from calling the high priests and rulers into His ranks. He gave the nation's sovereign the cold shoulder, and He did not invite men of distinction. He journeyed through the wilderness, through hamlets and market towns, and selected the poorest and the most wretched beggars He could find, such as poor fishermen and good, simple, uncouth bumpkins. It almost seems as though He felt unable to administer His kingdom unless He surrounded Himself with such simple folk. The great aristocrats He left behind in Jerusalem, although everybody assumed that the Messiah someday would associate with the bigwigs in Jerusalem, with the sages and the scholars. But Christ did the very opposite; He pursued His own plan and initiated His kingdom with such absurd simplicity as certainly to offend all wise men. (AE 22:189)

Philip confesses that Jesus of Nazareth is the one spoken of by the Law and the Prophets. In other words, Philip bears testimony to Jesus in accordance with the Scriptures of God. It was about Jesus that Moses wrote! It was about Jesus that the prophets preached! As we sing in the Christmas hymn:

> This is He whom seers in old time
> Chanted of with one accord,
> Whom the voices of the prophets
> Promised in their faithful word.
> Now He shines, the long-expected;
> Let creation praise its Lord
> Evermore and evermore. (*LSB* 384:3)

Our confession of Christ Jesus is never independent of the Holy Scripture. God's Scripture, which "cannot be broken" (Jn 10:35), bears witness to Christ, who alone is both Lord and Servant of the Scripture. Any confession of Christ that runs counter to the words of Scripture is "a different gospel" (Gal 1:6) and as such it is to be rejected as counterfeit. Our stance is always that of the Bereans in Acts 17 who "received the word with all eagerness, examining the Scriptures daily to see if these things were so" (Acts 17:11). Philip delivers the Gospel to Bartholomew in accordance with the Scriptures: "We have found Him of whom Moses in the Law and also the prophets wrote, Jesus of Nazareth" (Jn 1:45).

Bartholomew was less than sure about Philip's bold announcement. Skeptic that he is, he replies, "Can anything good come out of Nazareth?" (Jn 1:46). How could the Messiah come from such an insignificant place? But then, the God and Father of our Lord Jesus Christ is the God who elects to use "what is low and despised in the world, even things that are not, to bring to nothing things that are, so that no human being might boast in the presence of God" (1 Cor 1:28–29). God can use Nazareth, out-of-the-way town that it is, to be the hometown of His Son, just as He chose a peasant girl named Mary to be His mother. God gives us the treasures of His mercy and grace "in jars of clay, to show that the surpassing power belongs to God and not to us" (2 Cor 4:7).

God packs His Word with His own power. "By the word of the Lord the heavens were made, and by the breath of His mouth all their host" (Ps 33:6). That Word that goes forth from the Lord's lips does indeed accomplish His own purpose and plan. Long before the Word was on Philip's tongue or in Bartholomew's ear, the prophet Isaiah wrote, "So shall My word be that goes out from My mouth; it shall not return to Me empty, but it shall accomplish that which I purpose, and shall succeed in the thing for which I sent it" (Is 55:11).

Jesus' words "are spirit and life" (Jn 6:63). Filled with the Lord's own vitality, they create faith in the heart and confession on the tongue. The mighty words of the Lord, spoken by His servant Philip, bring Bartholomew to confess of Jesus,

"Rabbi, You are the Son of God! You are the King of Israel!" (Jn 1:49). Bartholomew the skeptic becomes Bartholomew the apostle.

Bartholomew was astonished by Jesus' words, "Before Philip called you, when you were under the fig tree, I saw you" (1:48). Our Lord assured Bartholomew that he would witness even greater things than this display of His perfect knowledge, for he would "see heaven opened, and the angels of God ascending and descending on the Son of Man" (1:51).

What could they mean, these strange words of Jesus? Our Lord's words echo the story of an Israelite in whom there was guile: Jacob. Before the Lord promised blessing to Jacob at Bethel, Jacob had a dream in which he saw a stairway (or ladder) connecting earth and heaven, and there "the angels of God were ascending and descending on it" (Gen 28:12). When Jacob awoke from his sleep he declared, "How awesome is this place! This is none other than the house of God, and this is the gate of heaven" (28:17).

Bartholomew sees "the house of God . . . the gate of heaven" in the flesh of Jesus. The Son of Man is the location of the glory of God. He is glorified, that is, He is lifted up on the tree of the cross to atone for the sins of the world so that all who look to Him in faith might live. These are the "greater things" (Jn 1:50) that Bartholomew would see.

Bartholomew would see these things, and he would be sent by the Lord Himself as an apostle to declare this Gospel to the nations. Bartholomew would spend his life in the service of our Lord and His Gospel. The glorious things that Bartholomew would see and hear would include the suffering and death of the Son of Man, the King of Israel. The Lamb of God who takes away the sins of the world carries them to the cross. There would be cross-bearing for Bartholomew also. According to the tradition of the Early Church, Bartholomew carried the Word of the cross to Asia Minor, Mesopotamia, Persia, and India, and then was flayed alive in Albanus. For that reason, the symbol for Bartholomew in ecclesiastical art is a knife.

The cost of confession is high! God grant that we, like Bartholomew, may confess Christ regardless of the cost.

Rev. John T. Pless

September

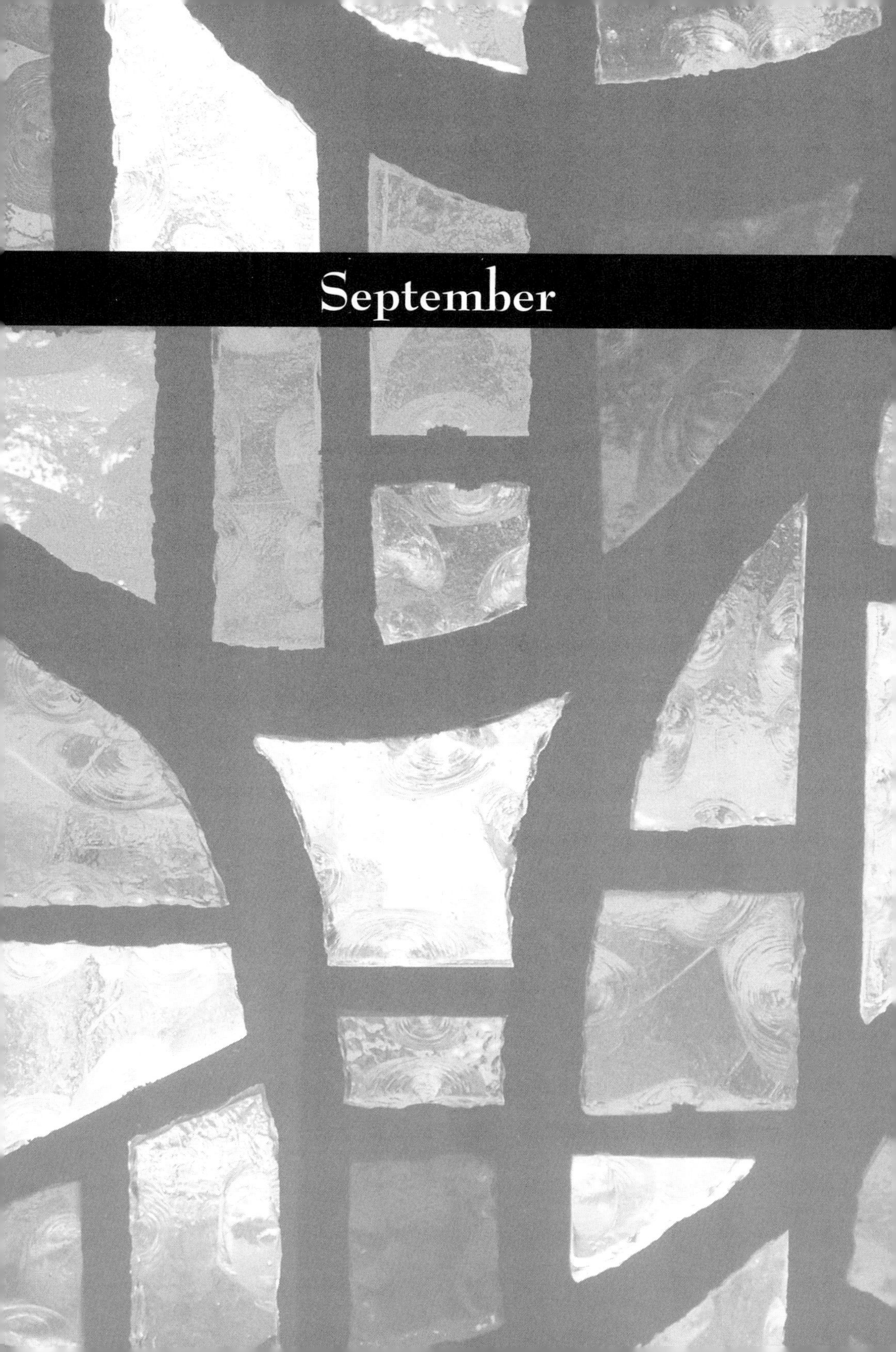

Holy Cross Day

The Glory of the Cross

John 12:20–33

On the day that Christ died, no one standing by would have spoken of the glory of the cross. At the cross, there was cruelty, unspeakable suffering, blood, darkness, and death. Yet we celebrate the cross with Holy Cross Day. We sing "Lift High the Cross." We are bold to speak of the glory of the cross. How can we do this? How can we speak of glory in the cross?

What is the glory of the cross? Jesus tells us. He tells us so that we might behold His true glory and glory in the cross of our Lord Jesus Christ.

Glory surrounds the cross. Although the word *cross* does not appear in today's Gospel, the cross is at the center of the text. Jesus talked about His coming death on the cross when He said, "And I, when I am lifted up from the earth, will draw all people to Myself." To these words John adds the comment, "He said this to show the kind of death He was going to die" (vv. 32–33). Jesus was to die by being lifted up on a cross.

To attach the word *glory* to the word *cross* seems absurd. The cross was the instrument of torture and death for criminals. Yet Jesus Himself speaks of the glory of the cross. In connection with the cross Jesus speaks of Himself as being glorified and of His Father being glorified. It becomes clear that glory surrounds the cross.

By the cross the Son is glorified. The request of the Greeks to see Jesus seems to have moved Him to think and talk about His suffering, death, and resurrection (vv. 20–23). At any rate, Jesus began to say, "The hour has come for the Son of Man to be glorified" (v. 23). Then He made clear that He was talking about His death. He did this by speaking of dying as the way to life. He observed that it is necessary for a kernel of wheat to be planted in order to bring forth many seeds (v. 24). "The death of Christ was the death of the most fertile grain of wheat" (Augustine).

Jesus spoke of what was about to happen in His life in terms of His glorification. He said that what would take place would show His glory. It would manifest His true splendor, majesty, and power as the Son of God.

The death of Jesus was glorification because of the meaning of that death and all that necessarily followed. He died to give us life with God (v. 24) and to drive out Satan, the prince of this world (v. 31). What followed the cross was obviously associated with the cross—His glorious resurrection and ascension. Jesus' cross was something much different than an instrument of shame, torment, and death. As St. Paul writes, Jesus "humbled Himself by becoming obedient to the point of death, even death on a cross. Therefore God has highly exalted Him and bestowed on Him the name that is above every name" (Phil 2:8–9). Glory truly surrounded the cross.

By the cross, the Father was glorified. As Jesus faced the torment of His death and His heart was troubled, He didn't pray to be saved from His hour of suffering but for the Father to glorify His own name (vv. 27–28). In response to this prayer the Father answered from heaven, "I have glorified it, and I will glorify it again" (v. 28).

The Father had already glorified His name throughout the ministry of Jesus. When Jesus proclaimed and taught the kingdom of God, healed the sick, fed the hungry, and raised the dead, He manifested the splendor of the Father's power, grace, and love. He glorified the Father's name.

Now the Father's name would be glorified again as Jesus made it possible for the Father to do what the Father wanted most to do—to show His love for people by forgiving sins and drawing people to Jesus for life and salvation. Truly, the Father's greatness, power, love, and goodness were displayed and seen in all their brilliance in the death, resurrection, and ascension of His Son, Jesus. Glory truly surrounded the cross.

We share in the glory of the cross. Jesus assures us that we share in the glory of the cross. We share in all that His death, resurrection, and ascension mean and offer.

We are able to live lives that have eternal value. Jesus said, "Whoever loves his life loses it, and whoever hates his life in this world will keep it for eternal life" (v. 25). Our faith relationship with Jesus, by which we have forgiveness of sins and the new and eternal life of the Holy Spirit, empowers us to live contrary to our sinful interests and desires that cause us to lose our lives. Instead, we are able to live lives of daily repentance that lead to eternal life. This is a life of sharing in the glory of the cross.

Jesus goes on to say more about the glory of our relationship with Him. "If anyone serves Me, He must follow Me; and where I am, there will My servant be also. If anyone serves Me, the Father will honor him" (v. 26). To hate our life in this world and keep it for eternal life involves serving and following Jesus. Living in a faith relationship with Him, we are His servants with whom He shares His heavenly glory. In His goodness and for Jesus' sake the Father honors us. We share in the glory of the cross.

We celebrate the glory of the cross. We celebrate the glory of the cross because Jesus of the cross has drawn others and us to Him just as He promised (v. 23).

Placing our faith in Jesus, we have the forgiveness of sins, life, and salvation, for He was lifted up to suffer the punishment for our sins and to be our victorious Savior.

> [The cross] is not destructive, repulsive, or punitive, it is attractive. It draws. As the sun draws the vapors of the sea, and then paints a rainbow on them, so Christ draws men, and then glorifies them. His attraction is like that of the sun. It is magnetic too, like that of the magnet to the pole. . . . It is not simply the Christ that is the magnet; it is the crucified Christ. It is crucifixion that has given him his attractive power, just as it is death that has given him his life-giving power. It is not Christ without the cross; nor the cross without Christ; it is both of them together.[4]

This time of celebration gives us the opportunity to repent. The very message of the cross gives us the reason and power to repent. And truly we need to repent for all the times we have put our self-centered and self-serving desires ahead of serving Jesus of the cross. We have flirted much too often with losing our lives rather than keeping them for eternal life. We need to remember every day of our lives and on the last day of our lives that dying is the way of life for the Christian just as it was for Jesus. We remember how it is with the grain of wheat that dies in the ground. It brings forth life.

Ignatius of Antioch went to a martyr's death, and in doing so he gave us an example of how a servant is to follow Jesus. As he suffered martyrdom, Ignatius cried out, "I am God's grain." Ignatius was willing to hate his life in this world in order to live eternally.

Did the Greeks who wanted to see Jesus actually get to see Jesus? If they did, and if they heard Jesus speak the words of the text, they saw what we see in today's Gospel. They saw the glory of the cross and, like us, gloried in the cross of our Lord Jesus Christ. We are drawn to the cross and to life by Jesus uplifted on the cross. God forbid that we should glory except in the cross of our Lord Jesus Christ.

Rev. Charles T. Knippel

---

4   Horatius Bonar (p. 145), taken from *Treasury of Quotations of Religious Subjects* © 1977 by F. B. Proctor. Published by Kregel Publications, Grand Rapids, MI. Used by permission of the publisher. All rights reserved.

October

St. Luke, Physician in the Truth

Luke 1:1–4; 24:44–53

The apostle Paul (Col 4:14) calls him "the beloved physician"—this evangelist whose day we are gathered to celebrate. Who was he, this man we know as St. Luke? He was a Gentile, well-schooled in the learning of the world. More important, he was one given the message of the Gospel to proclaim by writing an "orderly account" (Lk 1:3) of the things concerning our Lord Jesus Christ, so that Theophilus and millions of others—including you—would "have certainty concerning the things you have been taught" (v. 4). He was a traveling companion of Paul; he sticks with Paul to the end, as the apostle notes in today's Epistle, "Luke alone is with me" (2 Tim 4:11). So today the Church throughout the world praises the Lord and Giver of life for St. Luke, the evangelist, who was a physician in the truth.

St. Luke so writes that we might be healed by the truth that is the Son of God. St. Luke went to the sources, to "those who from the beginning were eyewitnesses and ministers of the word" (v. 2). St. Luke is a servant of that Word; he is no creative writer devising a moving story about a religious hero. He goes to those who heard with their own ears the voice of the Word made flesh. He traces his leads back to those whose eyes saw the Savior of the world. His Gospel is genuinely apostolic: from the apostles. His report issues from those who were there and whose testimony is sure. As the apostle John wrote:

> That which was from the beginning, which we have heard, which we have seen with our eyes, which we looked upon and have touched with our hands, concerning the word of life—the life was made manifest, and we have seen it, and testify to it and proclaim to you the eternal life, which was with the Father and was made manifest to us—that which we have seen and heard we proclaim also to you, so that you too may have fellowship with us; and indeed our fellowship is with the Father and with His Son Jesus Christ. And we are writing these things so that our joy may be complete. (1 Jn 1:1–4)

Luke writes that Theophilus might know the truth of the things of which he had been informed. Luke writes that Theophilus might know Jesus and the truth of His life, death, resurrection, and ascension. That truth, Dr. Luke knows, is the medicine of life. To know that truth is to have life in Jesus' name. No wonder that the Collect of the Day teaches us to pray:

> Almighty God, our Father, Your blessed Son called Luke the physician to be an evangelist and physician of the soul. Grant that the healing medicine of the Gospel and the Sacraments may put to flight the diseases of our souls that with willing hearts we may ever love and serve You; through Jesus Christ, Your Son, our Lord, who lives and reigns with You and the Holy Spirit, one God, now and forever. (*LSB Altar Book*, p. 980)

St. Luke proclaimed the truth of Jesus for the healing of souls made sick by sin. He writes his Gospel so that "all flesh shall see the salvation of God" (3:6). Our Lord is the Savior of the world, so St. Luke quite naturally traces His genealogy back to Adam. All of Adam's descendants are diseased and so in need of a Savior.

The salvation that is in Christ extends "far as the curse is found" (*LSB* 387:3) to use the words of the familiar Christmas carol. Thus the Christmas angels sing in their Gloria: "Glory to God in the highest, and on earth peace among those with whom He is pleased!" (2:14). In the Nunc Dimittis, Simeon blesses the infant Jesus, saying that his eyes have now seen the salvation that God has "prepared in the presence of all peoples, a light for revelation to the Gentiles" (2:31–32). Luke's "orderly account" includes two illustrations of God's mercy upon non-Israelites in the Old Testament: the widow of Zarephath and Naaman the Syrian (4:25–27). St. Luke's Gospel provides us with the account of our Lord's answer to the centurion's request for healing on behalf of his sick servant. Of that centurion, our Lord says, "I tell you, not even in Israel have I found such great faith" (7:9). As in the Great Commission of St. Matthew's Gospel, so also in St. Luke our Lord's parting words to His disciples at His ascension bid them to carry His Gospel "to all nations" (24:47). The healing balm of the Gospel proclaimed by Luke the evangelist and physician is for the whole world.

None are beyond the scope and power of that mighty Word. Mary's Magnificat rejoices in her God and Savior, who "has scattered the proud in the thoughts of their hearts" and "has brought down the mighty from their thrones and exalted those of humble estate" (1:51–52). After all, it was to humble shepherds that the high angel of God brought the announcement of the one who is born to be your Savior. Luke's Gospel is replete with examples of our Lord's care for the rejected and despised of this world.

In His hometown of Nazareth, our Lord sets the stage for the delivery of divine healing with His "messianic manifesto" drawn from Isaiah 61:

> The Spirit of the Lord is upon Me, because He has anointed Me to proclaim good news to the poor. He has sent Me to proclaim liberty to the captives and recovery of sight to the blind, to set at liberty those who are oppressed, to proclaim the year of the Lord's favor. (Lk 4:18–19)

To those people gathered for the Sabbath service in the synagogue at Nazareth, our Lord declares that this prophecy has been fulfilled in their ears. The remainder of St. Luke's Gospel documents the facts of this gracious fulfillment in the words and works, the parables and miracles of Jesus.

St. Luke gives us a "narrative," an "orderly account" of our Lord's journey to Jerusalem, where He embraced death on the cross for our redemption. Redemption is the theme of St. Luke's Gospel from beginning to end. Luke records the words of Zechariah's song as the old priest blesses "the Lord God of Israel, for He has visited and redeemed His people" (1:68). That redemption is won by Jesus Christ. He is the Lord who brings salvation to sinners like Zacchaeus, for He is "the Son of Man [who] came to seek and to save the lost" (19:10).

The salvation of the lost has a price: the suffering and death of the Son of God. St Luke, in his Gospel, diagnoses the disciples' malady: they did not understand that it was necessary that the Messiah should suffer and die:

> And taking the twelve, [Jesus] said to them, "See, we are going up to Jerusalem, and everything that is written about the Son of Man by the prophets will be accomplished. For He will be delivered over to the Gentiles and will be mocked and shamefully treated and spit upon. And after flogging Him, they will kill Him, and on the third day He will rise." But they understood none of these things. This saying was hidden from them, and they did not grasp what was said. (18:31–34)

St. Luke shows us that the death of the Great Physician was necessary to remedy the sins of the world. Nothing less would do!

Easter's empty tomb is the Father's assurance that His Son's death is remedy enough for the world's sins. St. Luke does not stop with the open tomb; he moves on to show us the risen Lord alive and active with His disciples, opening their minds to understand the Scriptures and making Himself known in the breaking of the bread. The risen Lord calls and gathers His own around His Word and Meal. Having so gathered His disciples, He then sends them to proclaim repentance and forgiveness of sins to all nations in His name. St. Luke ends his Gospel as he began it: on a note of blessing and joy, for Mary's Son is in truth the Son of God. Crucified and risen from the dead, He is the Savior of the world, our Savior. St. Luke rejoiced to give us a faithful and true record of that salvation. Today, the feast of St. Luke the evangelist, we rejoice in his Gospel and pray to God that we may be found faithful to its truth and healing power.

Rev. John T. Pless

St. Simon and St. Jude, Apostles

Called to Faith, Sent to Serve

John 14:21–27

Imagine yourself one of the twelve disciples, just after the start of spring. It's a clear April night after the rainy season has ended, with the hillsides green and the almonds blossoming. Christ has brought His little band together to fulfill the Passover Seder and transform it into the new covenant meal—the Lord's Supper.

You've been with Christ for three years now, wandering up and down Galilee, Samaria, and Judea; listening to Him teach and preach; watching Him heal the sick, raise the dead, and give sight to the blind. You've felt the tension of some of the religious leaders and the resentment against the Roman occupiers.

All of you have been concerned about coming to Jerusalem, the site of the temple, during Passover time. Rumors have been flying about how the scribes, Pharisees, and Sadducees want to do away with this religious teacher who has caused too much commotion by all His teaching and miracles, most of all by raising Lazarus.

You are gathered in a bare second-story room. The tomb of David is nearby. Shortly the Passover will end, and Christ will lead His band down the stone steps and sharp slopes to the Valley of the Kidron, and then up to Gethsemane on the Mount of Olives.

Among the twelve disciples for the Passover tonight are stalwart but emotional Peter; Judas Iscariot, who in a few hours will betray the Lord; and the beloved John, in whom Christ could most closely confide. But also among the disciples are two who are not well known, whose festival we are celebrating today: Simon and Jude. Each has a few mentions in Scripture, but in general they seem to have been more followers than leaders. Maybe we can identify with them even more closely than with Peter or John.

Biographies

Simon the apostle is mentioned in the tenth or eleventh spot in the lists of the Twelve. He is also called Simon Zelotes, Simon the Canaanite, and Simon the Zealot to differentiate him from Simon Peter. The Aramaic word wrongly translated as "Canaanite" also means "zealot"—whether for political activities or faith, we do not know.

He probably did not come from Canaan or Cana, where one tradition makes him the bridegroom at the changing of water into wine. He is carefully distinguished from Simon Peter and from the Simon who was a brother of Jesus. By tradition he served as a missionary all over the Near East, usually as a companion of Jude Thaddeus. The apocryphal Acts of Simon and Jude was a popular book in the Early Church. By tradition he died a martyr by being sawed in two, and in Church art he is often represented by a saw.

The Jude who is mentioned in the lists of the disciples in Luke and Acts appears as Thaddeus in Mark and Matthew, and as Lebbeus in several variant readings. In the Scriptures generally, and in this text, he is carefully distinguished from Judas Iscariot. By early tradition he was considered to be the brother of James, the brother of the Lord, and also the author of the Epistle of Jude. This apostle worked in Persia and Mesopotamia. By tradition he was martyred on the same day as Simon by a halberd—a combination battle-ax and spear, which often appears in paintings or stained glass that depict Jude.

How We Come to Faith

Thanks to St. John, we can overhear those warm words of Jesus known as the Upper Room discourse. Christ knew He would soon be leaving the disciples. This night again He taught them humility and service by washing their feet. Now He's summing up all His teaching to prepare them for going out into the world on their own.

He begins (v. 21), "Whoever has My commandments and keeps them, he it is who loves Me." The Greek words *entolas* and *tērōn* might better be translated "teachings" and "keeps watch over them." The point is that Jesus wants attention paid to what He has demonstrated, taught, and preached. Sentimental attachment isn't enough. Neither is blind church loyalty or a good record as a follower of the Torah or being charitable. Jesus is speaking of faith in Himself and of lives that reflect that faith.

How these disciples came to faith varied. Andrew was a disciple of John the Baptist who heard Christ teach. He brought his brother, Simon Peter. James and John were with their fisherman father, Zebedee, when they were called.

We today may be called to faith in varying circumstances. Many of us were baptized into Jesus at a very early age. The faith given us in Baptism was nourished as we learned more of Christ from a faithful mother or father or at Sunday School. Perhaps others first read of Christ during grade school days or sang the songs that tell of Him. Still others may have been called to faith as adults, perhaps when a personal crisis forced a reevaluation of life's meaning and purpose.

As Christ says, we should pay attention to what He has taught and who He is, what He stands for, and what He has done. He promises, "He who loves Me will be loved by My Father, and I will love him and manifest Myself to him" (v. 21).

But Jude or Judas—the same Jude whose festival we are celebrating today, who usually is rather reserved—breaks into the conversation and asks why Jesus has shown Himself primarily to the disciples and not to the whole world.

How Father, Son, and Spirit Work in Us

Christ expands His previous answer. First you must keep watch over the teachings I have been expounding. Through them you will have not only information but also life with God—the indwelling of Father, Son, and Holy Spirit. "If anyone loves Me, he will keep My word, and My Father will love him, and We will come to him and make Our home with him. . . . And the word that you hear is not Mine but the Father's who sent Me" (vv. 23–24).

So far, Jesus has been speaking of the here and now, in that Upper Room or Cenacle. Now He thinks of Pentecost, which is to occur right in that same structure in little more than fifty days. "The Helper, the Holy Spirit, whom the Father will send in My name, He will teach you all things and bring to your remembrance all that I have said to you" (v. 26).

As Luther explained the Creed's Third Article, it's the Holy Spirit who brings us to faith, enlightens us, and gathers us together to keep us in the true faith. It's no credit to us. We don't even get credit for reaching out our hand to accept the divine gift of grace. Only God does. Only the Holy Spirit. As Paul said to the Galatians, "You receive the Spirit . . . by hearing with faith" (Gal 3:2). The Spirit brings us the message of Jesus Christ, and He Himself accompanies the message with His presence, with His power, with His life.

Our sinful nature never really disappears, though the Holy Spirit over time does steer us in a lifestyle of obedience that is continually more God-pleasing. This we call sanctification.

The whole notion of living with God the Father, Son, and Holy Spirit in the very mystical closeness Jesus describes in His High Priestly Prayer gives us the comfort and confidence that God really is for us, dwelling in us, forgiving us and directing us.

Final Blessing and Commission

The disciples were already fearful of what might happen over the weekend of the Passover. Would Christ die? They needed His assurance and presence even more than usual.

Before the night was over, stalwart Peter would deny Him thrice, Judas would betray Him, and the rest would flee and lock themselves up—possibly in this very Upper Room where they were now meeting. Christ knew the disciples would be upset by what would soon take place: the betrayal, the denial, the crucifixion, the burial. But this was all part of the plan to empower the apostles with His power, now that He was nearer His time to return to heaven. After the resurrection and the ascension and outpouring of the Holy Spirit, courage and energy would return in superhuman measure.

Christ would not leave His disciples comfortless. He says, "Peace I leave with you; My peace I give to you. Not as the world gives do I give to you. Let not your hearts be troubled, neither let them be afraid" (v. 27).

Passing the peace has always been part of the culture of the Near East. *Shalom*, *salaam*, Hebrew or Arabic: peace. Peace be with you. One says it whether he is arriving or leaving. The phrase "Peace be with you" occurs more than a dozen times in the Scriptures. But when Jesus says it, He backs up the word with His life, His death, and His resurrection. He truly has peace to give us. Along with His message of peace, He and the Father and the Spirit come and live with us in an eternal life of love and peace.

In a way Christ's leave-taking is much like the ending of the liturgy. The time of teaching has ended, but the service is not over. The Lord is with you. Go in peace! Serve the Lord.

Rev. T. J. Kleinhans

Reformation Day

"For Us Fights the Valiant One"

Psalm 48

I live at the southeast corner of Lake Michigan. On a clear day I can see the skyline of Chicago, some thirty miles away, across the open waters. The silhouette of the Sears Tower, rising a little more than one thousand feet above its foundation, dominates the skyline. The tower is impressive. And if you are so bold as to set sail from our beach to Chicago without having a compass on board, all you have to do is point in the direction of that impressive sight: the Sears Tower.

If you have ever approached Jerusalem, almost three thousand feet above sea level, ascending from Jericho in the Jordan River Valley almost 1,300 feet below sea level, you will never forget the experience. The sight inscribes an indelible impression on your consciousness. Yes, it is easy to see why Jerusalem has been called the "city fair and high" (*LSB* 674:1), whose towers rise majestically above the surrounding landscape. Jerusalem, "the city of our God" (Ps 48:1), inspires pilgrims to sing.

Indeed, pilgrims did sing. For centuries they sang, especially those who were on their way from Galilee to the temple to celebrate the Feast of Passover or the Festival of the Atonement. Jesus and His disciples also made that trip on a number of occasions. They, too, likely were impressed as they made the ascent from the hot, stifling climate of the Jordan into the clear and fresh atmosphere of Jerusalem. It is enough to make one sing—as did the sons of Korah, the temple choir in ancient Jerusalem:

> Great is the LORD and greatly to be praised in the city of our God! His holy mountain, beautiful in elevation, is the joy of all the earth, Mount Zion, in the far north, the city of the great King. . . . Walk about Zion, go around her, number her towers, consider well her ramparts, go through her citadels, that you may tell the next generation that this is God, our God forever and ever. He will guide us forever. (Ps 48:1–2, 12–14)

HISTORICAL SITUATION

Psalm 48 is part of a trilogy of psalms (46, 47, 48) that sing God's praise because He had so wonderfully delivered His people—especially the holy city of David with the temple on Mount Zion, the oldest part of Jerusalem—from imminent danger.

This psalm contains few clues about the historical situation during which it was written, except that it is by the sons of Korah. Their forefather, a Levite, had rebelled against Moses and Aaron, and he, along with most of his relatives, were swallowed up by the earth (Num 16:1–49; 26:9–11; 27:3; Jude 11). However, a few did not join in his rebellion, and they were spared. Many generations later some of his descendants were appointed by King David to be singers, gatekeepers, and bakers in the temple (1 Chron 6:33–38; 9:19, 31; 15:17; 16:41, 42; 25:4–5; 26:19). Probably those "sons of Korah" in the temple choir were the ones who composed the eleven psalms that bear their name (Psalms 42; 44–49; 84; 85; 87; 88).

Many times in Jerusalem's history the city was protected by God in the manner suggested by Psalm 48. One instance occurred not long after Assyria destroyed the northern kingdom of Israel (722 BC). This story serves as an illustration of what the psalmist is singing about.

An Assyrian emperor by the name of Sennacherib led an expeditionary force of several hundred thousand soldiers in an attempt to subjugate Egypt. While besieging some of the Egyptian frontier forts that were located near what is today known as the Gaza Strip, Sennacherib sent a portion of his troops to take the city of Jerusalem (ca. 701 BC). He would not be satisfied with tribute. As long as Jerusalem existed as a fortified and independent city, it was an affront to his power. He felt that he had to bring the royal city of Judah to its knees. (A full account of the events is found in both Isaiah 36–39 and 2 Kings 18–20.)

Now Hezekiah recently had carried out his own efforts at reformation. This Old Testament reformer had torn down the pagan altars to false gods that dotted the countryside. With Luther-like courage, he braved fierce opposition and proclaimed that the people should worship at the altar of the one true God in Jerusalem.

The general in charge of Sennacherib's troops had instructions to taunt Hezekiah, the king of Judah, and to make fun of Hezekiah's God, the almighty Lord God of Israel. Speaking to all, the general said in effect, "Don't be tricked into believing that your God can save you. In fact, your God is mad at Hezekiah for tearing down the altars all over the countryside." (Obviously the general was confused about Hezekiah's reforms.) "Moreover, it was your God who ordered my boss, the king of Assyria, to destroy Jerusalem! We Assyrians have a long history of conquering other countries and humiliating the gods they worshiped. The gods of other countries have not been able to save them from us. Your God is no different than the others we have conquered. What makes you think He can save you?" (paraphrased from 2 Kings 18:19–35).

Needless to say, King Hezekiah was worried. So he consulted the great prophet Isaiah. God's spokesman told him not to budge. God would save the city, the king, and the people—not because they deserved it, but by His sheer grace (cf. Ps 48:9).

When Sennacherib's messengers reported back to him what Hezekiah's response was to the initial call for surrender, Sennacherib wrote an official ultimatum to Hezekiah. It reads as follows:

> Do not let your God in whom you trust deceive you by promising that Jerusalem will not be given into the hand of the king of Assyria. Behold, you have heard what the kings of Assyria have done to all lands, devoting them to destruction. And shall you be delivered? Have the gods of the nations delivered them, the nations that my fathers destroyed? (2 Kings 19:10–12)

When Hezekiah received the letter, he immediately went into the temple and spread the letter out on the floor: "Lord, do You see this? Are You going to let Sennacherib mock You this way? Yes, the Assyrians are powerful. But You can save us!" Then the prophet Isaiah came to Hezekiah and told him that God had heard his prayer. Jerusalem would be delivered.

A miracle happened. Shortly after all this had taken place, an angel of the Lord went through the camp of the Assyrian army outside the wall of Jerusalem, and—mysteriously—185,000 of the soldiers died. Sennacherib's army was decimated. Quickly and in disgrace he retreated home to Nineveh. While he was praying in his temple to the false god Nisroch, two of his sons assassinated him.

THE VICTORY TODAY

That is the end of Sennacherib's story. But the story of God's people goes on and on. God had saved His people, and once again He had shown that He is the Almighty. All other gods are as nothing; they only exist in the figment of human imagination. We deceive ourselves if we trust that which does not exist.

In much the same way, we are tempted to put our trust in ourselves or to rely on what we think we can accomplish. But in comparison to what God can do—to the power and might of God—the accomplishments of humanity are like straw and dust: sooner or later they are blown away, with nothing remaining behind.

This truth is one of the chief legacies of the Reformation: God alone is our sure defense. It is God who protects and defends us and who gives us victories out of His sheer grace in His Son, Jesus Christ.

The first and foremost victory of God is the victory over death. The time will come when we will pass out of this world. We can do nothing to prevent it. No matter how carefully we try to live, no matter what great care we take for our health and welfare, by our might can nothing be done. Unless Christ returns for us first, sooner or later we will all face the grave.

Nevertheless, for us fights God's valiant One, the very One whom God elected. This Messiah was promised from the very first day that death entered the spoiled Garden of Eden through the sin of Adam and Eve. With confident trust in the Christ, we sing in triumph with the sons of Korah and also with St. Paul:

> "Death is swallowed up in victory." "O death, where is your victory? O death, where is your sting?" The sting of death is sin, and the power of sin is the law. But thanks be to God, who gives us the victory through our Lord Jesus Christ. (1 Cor 15:54–57)

Jesus has fought the most important battle of all time for us. He stood face-to-face against the ultimate weapons of the devil: death and its cause, humanity's sin. Christ took both upon Himself. For a moment the devil must have thought that he had won; however, he was soon disappointed. For the very One whom he had wanted to get his hands on, the very One whom he had wanted to hold as a captive in the grave forever, rose on the third day! Jesus came back to life. He burst death's door. He split the grave wide open.

St. Paul was so impressed by this that once he came to know Jesus as his resurrected Savior, he never could get it out of his mind. He could preach nothing but Christ crucified and resurrected, victorious over the old evil foe. In Romans he sums it all up so well:

> Therefore, just as sin came into the world through one man, and death through sin, and so death spread to all men because all sinned. . . . But the free gift is not like the trespass. For if many died through one man's trespass, much more have the grace of God and the free gift by the grace of that one man Jesus Christ abounded for many. . . . If, because of one man's trespass, death reigned through that one man, much more will those who receive the abundance of grace and the free gift of righteousness reign in life through the one man Jesus Christ. (Rom 5:12, 15, 17)

LIVING THE VICTORY

The devil hates to give up, so he still assails us. He would still like to devour us. He shows his teeth, scowls, and growls at us. As Sennacherib did to Hezekiah, he makes all kinds of threats. Satan would be ever so happy if his threats were to wither our faith so that we would not trust the power of our God to help us. Satan wants us to give up and give in to him.

Therefore, we are in need of all sorts of smaller victories over him day by day. When temptations come, it is so easy to give in; it is so difficult to resist. It seems as if the devil has all the troops on his side. Like Sennacherib's army, which surrounded Jerusalem and made resistance seem pointless, so it seems as if the devil is irresistible. And it is true that without God's gracious help, our rate of success is not going to be above zero.

Nevertheless, faith is the hand that grasps God's promises, and we have a weapon in our hand. It is the sword of God's Word, the Word of God's promise: "And behold, I am with you always, to the end of the age" (Mt 28:20). Against even the briefest of God's promises, the devil is helpless.

When we were baptized, we were sealed with the Spirit and the mark of Jesus' cross. Our Lord proclaims that we are heirs of His victory, His victory for us in time and for eternity. Paul, in one of those mountaintop passages from the Bible, wraps it all up neatly when he says:

> Do you not know that all of us who have been baptized into Christ Jesus were baptized into His death? We were buried therefore with Him by baptism into death, in order that, just as Christ was raised from the dead by the glory of the Father, we too might walk in newness of life. . . . Our old self was crucified with Him in order that . . . we would no longer be enslaved to sin. . . . Now if we have died with Christ, we believe that we will also live with Him. . . . So you also must consider yourselves dead to sin and alive to God in Christ Jesus. Let not sin therefore reign in your mortal bodies, to make you obey their passions. (Rom 6:3–4, 6, 8, 11–12)

Therefore, we, too, can come into the presence of God, just as Hezekiah did. We can spread the insults of the world and the devil before the Lord. And we can turn to Him and claim His promise to deliver us from the evil that we by ourselves are unable to handle. Our individual and daily difficulties need not become stumbling blocks for us. We need not be intimidated by the threats and posturing of the devil, for victory now and forever is ours. It has become our inheritance by the strength of God's hand.

Therefore, our response can be just like that of the reformer Hezekiah and his people. We can sing a song of victory and make sure to "tell the next generation that this is God, our God forever and ever. He will guide us forever" (Ps 48:13–14).

Rev. David M. Albertin

Free to Live Unmasked

Romans 3:19–28

In the movie *The Mask*, Jim Carey's mild-mannered character becomes pretentious and extreme behind an ancient wooden mask. In *The Elephant Man*, a cloth hood protects the horribly disfigured title character from the beastly prejudice of others. Masks assist us in pretending to be who and what we are not. They also hide the shame of who and what we are.

On Halloween, we enjoy wearing masks. But on Reformation Day, we celebrate that we no longer need to hide behind them. For God has covered our sin and freed us to live unmasked lives in Jesus.

1. Free from pretense.
   A. The Jews hid behind their masks of righteousness and their works of Law, trusting these to merit favor with a holy God.
   B. Paul unmasks the Jews, stripping them of self-righteousness by the proclamation of the Law.
      (1) "So that every mouth may be stopped, and the whole world may be held accountable to God" (v. 19).
      (2) "No human being will be justified in His sight, since through the law comes knowledge of sin" (v. 20).
   C. We, too, are unmasked by the Law and are left standing naked before God in the judgment of sin. "For all have sinned and fall short of the glory of God" (v. 23).

Illustration: As Adam and Eve, once clothed with God's glory and likeness, found themselves naked and ashamed because of their sin, so we also are stripped of all pretense when we hear the voice of God in His Law. Our efforts to cover up our shame are useless. We are sinners. We are fallen. We are worms, no longer men (Ps 22:6). In the movie *The Elephant Man*, John Merrick attempted to hide his disfigurement beneath a fabric hood. But mere cloth could not conceal his huge, misshapen form. Our masks are just as useless. They may be more elaborate than fig leaves, but they are just as flimsy. They may seem innocent enough—claiming to be good, sincere, and upright before God and one another—but like Jim Carey's, our masks are proven by God's Law to be cartoonish, crass, and foolish.

Transition: The Law has the goods on us, doesn't it? By the Law, we understand that each of us stands naked and condemned before our God, not one of us excepted. But the Law is not the only thing we hear this morning, is it? While the

Law uncovers who we are by nature, the Gospel shows us who we are in Christ. While the Law reveals our ugliness, the Gospel clothes us in the righteousness of Jesus.

    2. Free from shame.
        A. A new righteousness has been revealed from God (v. 21).
            (1) It had its "bare bones" proclamation in the Law and Prophets (v. 21) but was "fleshed" out in Christ Jesus.
            (2) Christ covers our sin (v. 25), allowing sinners to stand bold and uninhibited before a gracious God.

Illustration: God provided Israel a testimony of His presence in the ark of the covenant topped by a mercy seat. By the annual smearing of blood on the mercy seat, Israel was assured that it could live within God's presence without fear. God also provides a mercy seat for us in Jesus (v. 25). Not only does His incarnation show that God is in our midst, but the shedding of His blood on the cross has covered our sin and hidden it from God. It is as if our nakedness were covered by Jesus, whose righteousness now guarantees that we can stand before our God and never be ashamed.

        B. This new righteousness is not by Law but comes by grace (v. 24) so that Christians do not have to be inhibited by doubt about how much they need to do to make God happy.
            (1) It was always by grace, even to God's people of the Old Testament who looked forward to the final Sacrifice that would be superior to that of bulls and goats.
            (2) It was by grace in the moment when the temple curtain tore in two, revealing Christ, the true mercy seat, to all who would believe.
            (3) It is still by grace, that is, the means of grace, as Jesus works within the "masks" of Word and Sacrament.

Transition: In much of our literature and movies, masks not only hide, but they also reveal. They are buffers that enable the unacceptable to be received by those who otherwise could not receive them. God also has clothed Himself in our humanity so that we poor sinners might receive a gracious God, a God who shields us from a glory that would be too much for us to bear. In Jesus, God puts on flesh and blood, and even wore our shame and died for it on a cross. Now, in Word and Sacrament, He comes to us that we might have a God who daily covers up our shame and frees us from pretense.

    3. Free to live unmasked.
        A. Before God.
            (1) We do not need to put on masks with God but can confess our sins and hear His promise: "I forgive you."

      (2) We do not need to be inhibited by fear or uncertainty but can come boldly before God in prayer, in the Divine Service, and in our daily living, because He sees us only in the righteousness of Jesus.

  B. Before our neighbor.

      (1) We do not need to pretend to be who we are not or add to who we are, but we can simply boast in being God's redeemed who gather, free of fear and all uncertainty, around our gracious God in Word and Sacrament (v. 27).

      (2) And we can confidently maintain to all—to our children, spouse, and neighbors—by the way we worship, speak, and serve, that "one is justified by faith apart from works of the law" (v. 28).

Conclusion: Halloween is for pretending to be something we are not and hiding who we are. But Reformation Day is for rejoicing in the person God has made and for celebrating all we have been given freely in Christ Jesus.

Rev. J. Richard Sawyer Jr.

Reformation Still Matters

Romans 3:21–24

Does the Reformation still matter? Do we really need a special service to remember what the Reformation was all about? Oh, I suppose it's helpful to remind us that Martin Luther is not the African-American civil rights leader from the 1960s! The Martin Luther we remember today is the man who lived in Germany some five hundred years ago and helped reform the Church. It's certainly useful for knowing who we are as Lutherans, a bit of our history. But does the Reformation really matter beyond that classroom exercise of keeping people straight and our tradition alive?

At first glance, the answer is no. You see, the Reformation wasn't so much about Martin Luther as it was about righteousness and certainty. How could we be right with God? How can anyone be certain of eternal life? Those were the questions the Reformation wanted answered.

In the United States today, most people aren't too concerned about those questions. An article by D. A. Carson in the magazine *Moody* says that most Americans don't think much about heaven or hell. In fact, most don't believe there is a literal place called hell. Neither do many believe there is a personal demonic being called Satan. As for heaven, not many get excited about the topic. The article says that we are not hungry, sick, or persecuted enough to look forward to a much better life. Life is pretty good in our country.[5]

AMERICANS ARE ETERNALLY OPTIMISTIC

But, of course, people still believe in life after death, which necessitates at least thinking about what will happen once you die. But when asked, just about everyone says they are going to heaven. Americans believe in happy endings. Americans are eternally optimistic. So if everything will ultimately turn out all right anyway, why worry about whether you're right with God or wonder how you can be certain about eternal life?

As an example of this happy optimism, after the terrorist attack on the World Trade Center, someone drew a picture of the buildings with the smoke billowing up and out. Out of the smoke were figures, people rising up to heaven. Standing above the smoke was Jesus, larger than the buildings, the smoke, and all the people. He had His arms open wide, welcoming everyone into His loving embrace.

---

5   D. A. Carson, "Living without Heaven or Hell," *Moody* (May/June 2001).

It's a wonderful picture, but is it accurate? Did everyone who died in that attack—except the terrorists, of course—end up in Jesus' loving arms and in heaven, as the picture seems to say? Does getting killed in a terrorist attack automatically qualify you for heaven?

No, not according to St. Paul in this Romans passage: "All have sinned and fall short of the glory of God" (Rom 3:23). He says that no matter who you are—a stockbroker, pilot, janitor, airline passenger, husband, wife, child, or friend—it doesn't matter how you die. It doesn't matter if you are young or old, sick or healthy, whether death came quickly or days later. It doesn't matter if death comes at the hands of a terrorist, a drunk driver, cancer, or old age. All are sinners. All have fallen short of the glory of God.

If we have all sinned and fallen short of God's glory, then who is welcomed in the arms of Jesus and who isn't? That is the very question that makes the Reformation so important. How can we be right with God so that I can be certain I'll end up in heaven? American optimism or wishful thinking just won't do. We need to know for sure, and that's why the Reformation still matters.

SCRIPTURE IS THE SOURCE

Those eternal questions were answered by Martin Luther and the other reformers by turning to God's own Word. Their answers were not made up to make everyone feel good nor guided by what most people believed. Rather, the Reformation answers were to stand on Scripture alone.

WE ARE JUSTIFIED FREELY THROUGH JESUS CHRIST

The Book of Romans was pivotal. We've already heard how all have sinned and have fallen short of the glory of God. But that's not the last word. Scripture adds that righteousness comes from God, that we are justified freely by God's grace through Jesus Christ, gifted with a new status, righteousness, free of all guilt before God.

Being right with God is His doing. Grace alone saves us. God reaches down with His amazing, unmerited grace and makes our relationship with Him right and good. Nothing of our own do we bring; only His unmerited love for us in Jesus, and Him alone, gives us the righteousness that we need for eternal life. That's where the picture about the terrorist attacks has it right. Standing above everything is Jesus. If anyone from that terrorist attack was going to heaven, it was because of Jesus. Perhaps I'm seeing more than what's really there, but in that picture I believe that His outstretched hands have nail marks in them. He hung on a cross to restore a right relationship between God and us. Eternal life comes from His death, and certainty comes from His resurrection. Jesus welcomes people with His loving, open arms because the grave could not hold Him. Death had no lasting power over Him. Only Christ our Savior can guarantee that life after death will bring heaven instead of hell, a loving Father instead of Satan.

Christ alone is the Reformation's answer, the Bible's answer, and God's answer to those questions of righteousness and certainty. And faith alone holds onto Jesus, onto God's grace in Him. Our faith stands on Scripture alone, grace alone, Christ alone. And this Reformation certainty about God's righteousness in Jesus still matters.

Recently five teenagers who were in my son's high school were in a horrendous automobile accident. Three of them were killed. Our 15-year-old son, Tim, knew the young girl who died. We've talked a couple of times about what happened, and one of his comments stands out for me. He said that the terrorist attacks were terrible, but this was something different. This death was personal. He knew her. He had talked to her. And now she was dead. This was personal, not something awful a thousand miles away.

When death—and life—get personal, too close to ignore, too near to rely on American optimism and wishful thinking, that's when the Reformation still matters. And the Reformation's answer to questions of righteousness and certainty in such personal and up-close moments is Jesus. That young girl is not in heaven because she died at a tender age or by accident, but because Jesus willingly died for her. God's grace reached into her life at Baptism, which connected her to Jesus' death and resurrection and gave her faith to hold onto Jesus. He brings her home to heaven safely.

My parents' cemetery is in central Wisconsin. When I stand in front of my mother's grave, I remember her faith. She took us to church. She loved to sing hymns. She filled her Bible with clippings and devotions. Her faith in Jesus was there for her children to see. But my father was a different story. He didn't go to church except for weddings and funerals or special occasions. We didn't see him pray or talk of Jesus. Oh, he was a good man who worked hard to provide for his family on a small farm in Wisconsin, but we saw little evidence of a relationship with his Lord.

About ten years before he died, my father suffered a severe stroke. We could take him places on occasion, but mostly he just sat at home playing solitaire, reading children's books, and watching television. I was in high school and college at the time. If I had made conclusions only on what I had seen before the stroke and his sitting in the chair, his death would have no happy ending.

But while I was in school, our pastor would stop by the house and visit with Dad. He would read from the Bible and tell him of Jesus. Then he'd bring out a little book that had an abbreviated Communion service in it. He'd walk my father through confession and absolution. He'd place the bread and wine, the body and blood of Jesus into his mouth. They'd say the Lord's Prayer together. He'd pronounce the benediction over my father. And God's grace was there. Jesus was there.

It's been twenty-five years since my father died. Yet I try to visit that cemetery each year. Each time I walk up to his grave, his death is still personal, and that's when the Reformation still matters. Without God's grace, I'd stand there with no hope. "For all have sinned and fallen short of the glory of God." But by God's grace alone, Jesus brings righteousness and life to someone like my father, and to people who have died in a terrorist attack, and to young people who get killed in automobile accidents, and to you and me. Yes, the Reformation still matters, for righteousness and certainty come from Jesus and Him alone.

Rev. Glenn A. Nielsen

Free to Serve

John 8:31–36

People today cry out for freedom. This surge for freedom brought down the Berlin wall, reunited Germany, broke up the Soviet Union, and brought the death of Communism, the welfare state, and the idea of a big government that does all the planning to save society from its ills.

The struggle for freedom—even spiritual liberty—is not new. Four hundred and seventy-one years ago many Christians in western European countries were waging a struggle for freedom from a huge institutional church that dominated their lives and told them what to believe and do. We call their struggle the Reformation. Martin Luther championed the cause for spiritual freedom made possible by God's grace in Jesus Christ. In 1520 he wrote *The Address to the German Nobility*, in which he attacked the Church's exercise of authority over governments. Two months later in *The Babylonian Captivity of the Church*, he attacked the Church's penitential system by which it controlled Christians.

Luther connected freedom with service to one's neighbor and the extension of God's kingdom. In November 1520, he published *The Freedom of the Christian*, in which he applied his evangelical theology of freedom in Christ to the daily Christian life of service. This tract echoes the words of Jesus in our text. This morning, then, we will address freedom—the freedom of the Christian but also the necessity for service and mission work—under the theme "Free to Serve."

Luther states two powerful principles. The first is:

1. A Christian is free, lord of all, subject to none.
    A. I can explain this with a remote but obvious point, namely, that you have a twofold nature, an outer and an inner self.
        (1) I recall visiting a family with a newborn child. All the relatives were gathered around and identified the parts. "He's got his mom's nose and his dad's chin. There is his grandpa's forehead." Inside, however, was a unique human spirit, a unique self that was really in bondage and slavery. If nothing intervened from the outside, by the time the child was twenty-one you would see the world's agenda, America's cultural values implanted in his mind and heart. He would be, as St. Paul declares, among the walking, living dead who follow "the prince of the power of the air," the devil, and who follow the desires of their own sinful nature (Eph 2:1–3).

(2) When Jesus proclaims to His followers that "if you abide in My word, you are truly My disciples, and you will know the truth, and the truth will set you free" (Jn 8:31–32), He gets a reaction from some Jewish followers that they had never been slaves. How could He set them free? Jesus responds by telling the truth: "Everyone who commits sin is a slave to sin" (v. 34).

Jesus is talking about the inside. Outwardly the Jewish people did not consider themselves slaves or subjects to anyone (though they were subject to the occupying Romans). Jesus has them look inside for human bondage.

B. If slavery and bondage to sin and death are inside, how are people set free? Wars? Revolutions? Legislative votes? Of course not! Those are all external. There are three aspects to how people are truly set free.

(1) The cause: God sent His Son, Christ Jesus, to take upon Himself our human nature. He identifies with us, yet He is without sinful bondage on the inside. Jesus is truly and completely free, yet He freely subjected Himself to our sin and death. He became sin for us so that in Him we might become the righteousness of God. Thus He puts our bondage to death. Yes, He puts death itself to death. His work changed God's attitude toward the whole world. Because of Christ, God is reconciled to the world. He forgives us and frees us from the wages and power of sin.

(2) The carrier: The word about the cause of freedom, namely, Christ crucified, is the great emancipation proclamation, the means by which the Holy Spirit works to connect people to Christ.

(3) The connection: The Holy Spirit works faith in the heart. This faith functions three ways:

  a. Faith receives the promise of the Gospel. Faith clings to and holds on to the forgiveness of sins and freedom from bondage to sin and death.

  b. Faith also unites a person with Jesus Christ. This union is like a marriage, in which all that belongs to the husband becomes the wife's and all that belongs to the wife becomes the husband's. My wife brought her qualities of organization, determination, and goodwill to the marriage, helping to overcome my qualities of foolishness, stupidity, and the like.

  Christ took on all your sin, your lust, your greed, your selfishness, your death, and in exchange, He gives you His life, His wisdom, His peace, His joy, His righteousness, His glory, His power. You abide in Christ, and He abides in you, just like a branch on a vine. As Paul declares, "It is no longer I who live, but Christ who lives in me" (Gal 2:20). With Jesus living in you, you are a new creation; you are free from sin and death. As Jesus declares, "If the Son sets you free, you will be free indeed" (v. 36).

   c. By faith you also exercise the power of freedom, the power of Christ Jesus, the power of being priests and kings and queens of God in the face of adversity, calamity, and life problems. It is not you who does this, but Christ Jesus living in you and through you. In Christ you are a free lord of all, subject to none on earth. Yet Luther also states a second, corresponding principle:

2. Luther's second principle is that a Christian is a dutiful servant of all, subject to all.

While we are united with Christ through faith, we also live in relation to family, to neighbors, to millions of world-class unbelievers, to a great variety of human cultures. It is here that our faith is put to work. We freely become obedient slaves to please God, without thought of gain, in love that is not constrained.

  A. A working, active faith makes us slaves in two ways.

    (1) Slaves of righteousness: Every day you read in the paper about murders and robberies, sexual harassment and child abuse, drunk drivers and drug dealers, or feuding neighbors and family violence. None of this should be found among Christians. We Christians have a much higher standard of ethics and morality. You are not to be conformed to your culture, but to discipline your nature, your values, your habits. By the power of the Holy Spirit, you are transformed into little Christs. Paul encourages you to put off the old self; to put to death falsehood, anger, gossip, envy, and the like; and to offer yourself to God as an instrument of righteousness. "Having been set free from sin," he says, "[you] have become slaves of righteousness" (Rom 6:18).

    (2) Not only are you slaves to righteousness, but also you are to act as slaves to your neighbors. Here God's Word directs your free inner self, in whom Christ dwells, to obey voluntarily and joyfully by loving your neighbors and your enemies, praying for those who persecute you, turning the other cheek, going the extra mile, giving your cloak to those who take your coat, putting your spiritual gifts

to work for the common good of the local and worldwide body of Christ. Here you are directed to serve freely by financially and prayerfully supporting the work of missionaries who bring the Gospel to many ethnic groups and individuals.

In response to the inquiry "Who is my neighbor?" Jesus spoke the parable of the Good Samaritan, which concludes with the question, "Which of these three, do you think, proved to be a neighbor to the man who fell among the robbers?" (Lk 10:36). The answer: the one who had mercy, the one who proved he was a neighbor by his actions. Jesus then spoke a booming "Go and do likewise." His words speak to you today. Don't just talk about being a loving neighbor or being concerned about sending missionaries. Go and do it!

B. Who is capable? Only the free can serve freely. Only those in whom Christ Jesus lives can "go and do likewise." He covers over sins and gives you His life, His mind, His love, His compassion, and His strength.

The good things of God should not only flow into you, but from you to your neighbor as you empty yourself, not abusing your freedom, but taking on the form of a servant to your neighbor, as you cover their sins and failures and pain and also labor for them as if they were your very own. That is what Christ did for you.

I conclude then that Christians live not in and for themselves, but in and for Christ Jesus and for their neighbor. You live in Christ through faith and for your neighbor in love. By faith you are caught up beyond yourself into God and are freed from sin and death. By love you move out of yourself, toward your neighbor to serve, yet you always remain in God's love in Christ. Through God's Son, you are free indeed!

Rev. Raymond L. Schiefelbein

Keep on Reforming!

Hebrews 13:7–9a

Some past events, like birthdays and anniversaries, are worth remembering. Important dates are highlighted on our calendar, and every year we remember them. The Lutheran Reformation is among those events most worth remembering. All who cherish the truthful proclamation of the Gospel of Jesus Christ, who alone grants the forgiveness of sins and eternal life, will want to remember the Reformation.

It was in Wittenberg, Germany, early in the sixteenth century, that sparks from Martin Luther's pen and tongue ignited the Reformation. The fire burned brightly and blazed three principles into church history—principles that are found in the Scriptures and have been known and believed in the Christian Church throughout the ages, even if at times they have been obscured. In Latin these three principles are *sola gratia, sola fides, sola Scriptura*; in English, grace alone, faith alone, Scripture alone. The Reformation is worth remembering, and as we preserve its memory, it is just as important that we continue it. So in the title of this sermon the verb "reform" is in the present tense and active voice: Keep on Reforming.

Let there be no misunderstanding. Our redemption is complete. The saving work of Jesus Christ was finished nearly two thousand years ago, and what He did is sufficient for the salvation of everyone who has ever lived on earth. That is the central doctrine of Scripture, and Martin Luther did not reform or tamper with it in any way. There is nothing to add to the work of Christ. But something is still needed: the work of Christ still must be proclaimed, confessed, and believed. It must shape the entire life of the Church and preserve us from fatal error. Therefore it must be said: in the name of Jesus, keep on reforming.

Hold on to these great Reformation truths: grace alone, faith alone, Scripture alone. That is our heritage—the heritage of all Christians everywhere and of all times, and the heritage preserved with unsurpassed clarity in the Lutheran Church. But ours is not to be just a polite remembering or an inflated remembering that borders on pride. Keep on reforming: that is to say, let God make continuous application of the three principles to our life as a corporate church and to your own personal life.

The continuing process of remembering and reforming is suggested in our text. *(Read Heb 13:7–9a.)* The text provides us with a clear outline for this process that we call reformation. It has three principles—not word-for-word the same as the three Reformation principles, but the three principles in the text involve or contain the three *solas* in this order: Scripture alone, faith alone, grace alone.

First, "Remember your leaders, those who spoke to you the word of God" (v. 7). Word-of-God leaders are worth remembering. Remember the faithful pastors and teachers, your parents and relatives, those who first brought you to Christ in Holy Baptism, according to the Word of God; who nourished your baptismal faith through instruction in the Word; and who, when you were prepared, brought you to the Table of the Lord to receive His body and blood, as He said: "Do this in remembrance of Me" (Lk 22:19). Remember also every brother or sister in Christ whose example or wise counsel or sincere encouragement brought the Word to bear upon your life. Remember and give thanks for Word-of-God leaders.

Where the Scriptures are read, where Christ's words to baptize and to celebrate His Supper are remembered—in those places the message is made personal and the Word of God is planted in hearts. In those places the Reformation continues. We worship the triune God who speaks to us through a book: Father, Son, and Spirit. The red stole and paraments today remember Pentecost, when the red flames of the Spirit first blazed. The Spirit works through the Scriptures, revealing to us our living Savior, full of grace and truth. A church in reformation is a church that believes His Word. We "read, mark, learn, and inwardly digest" the Word, "that we may embrace and ever hold fast the blessed hope of everlasting life" (*TLH*, p. 14). Keep on reforming, guided by the Scriptures alone!

Second, "imitate their faith" (v. 7). The faith of those spiritual leaders who speak the Word is worth imitating. As one who has ministered to many who are now in glory, I have gotten real shots of spiritual adrenaline from stalwart Christians who fought the good fight and finished the race. We learn what it means to walk by faith as we imitate those who live by faith—starting with our Lord Jesus Christ.

Admiration for my grandmother's faith or a sense of inspiration from observing my neighbor's faith in action is important, but it must be added to—not substituted for—my own faith in Christ. The righteous live by faith; those who live by faith are righteous. Now, faith is not a pious sentiment, a wishful thought, or a nice dream that disappears when we wake up and face reality. Faith is a gift, generated by the power of the Holy Spirit. Faith is the assurance of things hoped for. Faith is an unswerving trust in Him whom the Scriptures reveal: Jesus Christ. Faith clings to the Son of God despite all the uncertainty and change around us and in us. As Heb 11:1 says, "Faith is the assurance of things hoped for, the conviction of things not seen."

The object of our faith is the person and work of Jesus Christ. He is the central message of Scripture. Jesus Christ, God's Son and our Savior, "is the same yesterday and today and forever" (v. 8). He never changes! We are always changing. That is why we always need reformation and renewal. We change our mind. We change our appearance. Even if we do not want to change, year by year we grow older and the family album reveals the change. But the God of love, who has made Himself known to us in the flesh of His Son, Jesus—He never changes!

Christ offered Himself into death on the cross as the perfect sacrifice for all sin. He suffered to atone for the sin of everyone, the whole world. He won forgiveness for the sin we inherited from Adam and Eve, as well as for the sins we daily commit. Jesus, our great High Priest, is our advocate, interceding for us before the throne of His heavenly Father. He was crucified, raised from the dead, and now lives forever. He promises that we will live forever too. He will come again to receive us to Himself. Until that glorious day, living by faith alone, we keep on reforming!

Third, "do not be led away by diverse and strange teachings" (v. 9a). It is necessary, in the name of Jesus, to keep on reforming. Daily we need to be strengthened by grace. Regrettably, strange and diverse teachings are not in short supply. They are as accessible as the New Age section of our local bookstore, the wacky television talk shows, and the psychic hotlines. A church that is faithful to the Scriptures will always find itself in conflict with twisted minds and erring consciences. But if we are immersed in grace and continue in the means of grace—remembering our Baptism, hearing the Word, receiving our Lord's Supper—we will not be led astray. Through the Good News of the Gospel, the grace of the Lord Jesus Christ continues to strengthen us.

In Christ we are given those most expensive gifts that we desperately need. We refer to them as the forgiveness of sins, life, and salvation. They are prohibitively expensive, far more than we can afford, but they were charged to the account of Christ Himself. His blood paid the price. According to the Scriptures, these gifts are ours *gratis*, by grace, and for free, through faith. God gives them to us for the sake of Christ. This is the grace of our Lord Jesus Christ. St. Paul's declaration in Holy Scripture remains unchanged: "By grace you have been saved through faith. And this is not your own doing; it is the gift of God, not a result of works, so that no one may boast" (Eph 2:8–9). Strange and diverse teachings can only lead us astray to death. God's grace, coming to us through His Word and Sacraments, strengthens our hearts and leads us to life.

Grace alone, faith alone, Scripture alone—those three principles summarize the wonderful heritage of truth with which we have been blessed. But if we only extol the virtues of our past, we will become a stagnant pond. The Church today must continue to be a Church that gathers around the means of grace for worship. We must be a confessing Church, a baptizing Church, a communing Church; a serving Church, a rejoicing Church, a witnessing Church; a studious Church, a Church well grounded in grace alone, faith alone, Word alone.

It is easy to become complacent, lazy. Can we dig into the Word more than we have? Do we leave the Word alone rather than stand on the Word alone? Can we confess the faith more often and more boldly? Can we abound in grace more than we have? What about our attendance at worship, Holy Communion, Bible class?

Disturbing issues such as abortion, assisted suicide, and homosexuality cry out for life-affirming testimony and concern based on unchanging truth from the Scriptures alone. Confused and lonely persons need our understanding and compassion. Errors abound in the world—errors that we must challenge and counter with the Gospel. The hope for our despairing world is found only in Christ; only the Church has the answer. Reformation begins right here with you and me, as individual members of the Body of Christ. In the name of Jesus—keep on reforming!

Someone asked an elderly Christian gentleman who lived by himself, "What do you do with all your time?" The veteran saint answered, "I have much to do every day. I have two falcons to tame, two rabbits to keep from running away, two hawks to manage, a serpent to confine, a lion to chain, and a sick man to wait upon." Somewhat bewildered, this friend said, "You will have to explain that to me. No one has all these things to do at once." The old gentleman replied, "Indeed, I have all these things to do, for the two falcons are my two eyes, the two rabbits are my feet, the two hawks are my hands, the serpent is my tongue, the lion is my heart and the sick man is my own body."

Are there any among us who can say that the Reformation is complete in their life and in their church? Should we not, like that elderly Christian, alert the guards, secure the doors, and tighten the defenses lest Satan get the better of us and do his worst in us? Should we not also go on the offensive, combating error with truth and liberating those still held captive in darkness and confusion?

> Through toil and tribulation
> And tumult of her war
> She waits the consummation
> Of peace forevermore
> Till with the vision glorious
> Her longing eyes are blest,
> And the great Church victorious
> Shall be the Church at rest. (*LSB* 644:4)

In the name of Jesus—keep on reforming!

Rev. Randall W. Shields

Freedom from an Unsavory Slavery

John 8:31–36

A magnificent army had taken the field that late summer day. What a splendid display of martial might! The cavalry soldiers sat tall in the saddle, their regimental flags unfurling a rainbow of colors in the wind. Strong young men on foot stood ready for the order to advance. The spotless steel of the officers' drawn swords shone in the sun. The commander reviewed his troops with pride. This was a military force to be reckoned with. They were ready for battle and more—for victory!

The scene? Something out of the middle ages or Custer's last stand? No. That late summer day was scarcely fifty years ago, and the field of battle was a border in eastern Europe. The force described was the grand army of Poland, respected at the time as one of the world's finest. It stood bravely to defend its homeland. Across the border, however, an aggressor nation had massed a different type of army. Horses had been replaced by panzer tanks in the army of Nazi Germany. Its generals were about to unveil a new kind of warfare: Blitzkrieg, lightning war.

How did the two armies fare that summer day? According to the historian William Manchester, the Polish defenders charged the German lines, only to be mowed down by the German infantry and artillery, leaving more than a mile of mangled bodies. Those who survived were taken prisoner. The Polish survivors were seen hitting the tanks, proof that they had been told a lie when someone had said they were fakes made of cardboard.[6]

Someone had been wrong, indeed. The whole world had been wrong about the Nazi threat. Still remembering the horror of World War I, the nations of the world refused to believe that the Nazi juggernaut existed. Evidence of Hitler's intent abounded, but it was too unpleasant to acknowledge. In this act of denial we find exposed a tragic weakness in the human condition: we are easily deluded to accept as true that which we wish to believe is true. Wanting to believe that the Nazi armor was cardboard, the Poles were deluded into thinking a cavalry charge would win the day. Enslaved by their own delusion were those gallant soldiers that late summer day.

---

6   William Manchester, *The Last Lion: Winston Spencer Churchill, Alone 1932–1940* (New York: Dell, 1988), 574.

Perhaps it was another late summer day that the discussion between Jesus and the Jews recorded in our text took place. Self-delusion surely was a factor in this dialogue. Up to the point of our text the conversation proceeded fairly well. Some of the Jews had even agreed with Jesus on several of His teachings. However, the moment Jesus mentioned that His hearers were slaves, the course of the discussion took a turn for the worse.

"Slaves?" said the Jews. "We are offspring of Abraham and have never been enslaved to anyone" (Jn 8:33)—a dubious assertion, considering Israel's bondage in Egypt, the Babylonian exile, and the current Roman military occupation of Palestine. Yet Jesus had in mind a more important matter: not slavery to other human beings, but slavery to sin. "Everyone who commits sin is a slave to sin" (v. 34), Jesus said, an indictment that stands against all people.

If these Jews were not receptive to the idea that they had been enslaved by humans, they were even less receptive to the idea that they were slaves to sin. This Jesus was simply going too far. As Abraham's children, they were free. There was no need to be freed by anyone, and there was certainly no need to continue in the word of this upstart teacher. "We already are free," they insisted.

What a grand delusion! Evidence of their sinfulness abounded, but sin had so inflated their pride they could not accept the truth of Jesus' word. They were slaves to a power that had tricked them into thinking they were free. All slavery is bad, but particularly unsavory is this slavery to sin, a slavery that masquerades as freedom.

It's tempting for us to stand in judgment over these Jews, isn't it? It's easy to condemn them, as if we were better or smarter than they, as if we would never be so deluded. The temptation surely exists, but we would do well to resist it, for the truth of the matter is that we are just like them.

Like those Jews, we, too, will listen to Jesus about many things. We like to hear about eternal life, about God giving us daily bread, about Jesus being with us always. We even like the idea of His judging wicked people at the end. Yet when Jesus pushes into the sensitive areas of our lives, we want to turn Him off. When Jesus calls the scribes and Pharisees hypocrites, we cheer in agreement; but when He refers to our own hypocrisy of singing praise to God's name in church, and then using that same name to curse someone at home, we begin to thumb through the bulletin. When Jesus speaks of God's love for all people, we rejoice; but when He brings up our prejudice against those same people, we bring the discussion to a close.

It's not that we deny our sins. We're willing to admit we behave wrongly. But call us slaves? That's an insult. "I can stop doing that sin whenever I want. I just need to try harder—that's all. I can conquer it. I'm not enslaved; I'm in control of my life."

What a grand delusion! We are slaves of sin. We can't stop. In our natural state, sin is our master. To think otherwise is a delusion. That's why this slavery is so unsavory: it works to shield us from the truth of just how enslaved we are. We are like the inept prisoners who think they can tunnel their way to freedom. Smuggling a shovel into their cell, they dig and dig and dig; but bereft of blueprint or compass, their tunnel comes up in the cell next door. On their second attempt, they tunnel into the guard's room. On their third attempt, they tunnel into the warden's office. No matter how hard they try, no matter how many tunnels they dig, they haven't the means to succeed; they always come up still in prison.

So it is with our attempts to conquer sin ourselves; we haven't the means to set ourselves free. The result is always an unsavory slavery. As William Barclay put it, "The point is that the man who sins does not do what he likes; he does what sin likes."[7]

How we would like to be free, but sin holds us captive. Captives we would remain were it not for the boundless grace of our triune God. Seeing our wretched condition, our slavery to sin, God sent an emancipating Word, the incarnate Word, His holy Son. As the very Son of God, Jesus has the authority to free us from our unsavory slavery. He has led the charge to gain our freedom, not with an army of cavalry but with His life on Calvary. Although He committed no sin of His own, He allowed Himself to be made a prisoner of sin—your sin, my sin—on the cross. Although He was free to turn away from that hideous death at any time, He willingly offered Himself as the sacrifice. Spurning His own release, He bought freedom for the world with His holy, precious blood. For all our unsavory sins—even the most private sins we are reluctant to confess—Christ gave Himself; and by that gift we are freed from their damning curse.

If our freedom had resulted in the eternal loss of the guiltless Savior, it would have had a most unsavory flavor to it. There would be little joy over a liberty that left the Liberator dead. How sweet, then, is God's liberation. The Son of God remained not in bondage to death; He broke free of that prison. He arose to give new life to every believer. The triumphant Jesus ascended to God's right hand as King of kings and Lord over all.

In Baptism, Christ's gracious kingdom has extended to you. The heavy chains of your unsavory slavery to sin have been cast into the depths of those holy waters, taking your old, sinful self down with them. Out of that water the Spirit raises a new person, righteous and holy before the Father, not by your own deeds of obedience but by the freeing deeds of Jesus in your stead. You are unleashed from sin's shackles, a slave no more. In Baptism, the Son has set you free, and when the Son sets you free, you are free indeed!

---

7   William Barclay, *The Gospel of John* (Philadelphia: Westminster, 1956), 2:23.

Yet one chapter of our story needs finishing: your own. By the Gospel you have been set free from sin's unsavory slavery, but you will remain free only as the Word of life remains in you through faith. "If you abide in My word, you are truly My disciples, and you will know the truth, and the truth will set you free" (vv. 31–32). So spoke Jesus. This is the chapter that needs finishing—the one where you continue in Christ's Word, holding to Him in faith.

We do not face this task unopposed. Satan has not forgotten about us. Christ conquered sin on the cross, but the devil is still active. Daily he tempts us. Daily he speaks the lie that freedom means being your own master, not the servant of another. Daily sin works to enlarge our foolish pride so that it becomes harder to confess our trespasses. Daily the need for the Savior is obscured. Daily the battle to re-enslave us is waged. But Jesus provides the weapon for daily victory: His Word, which fortifies our faith in Him.

That's what Jesus meant by calling us to continue in His Word. Each day we cling to Him alone for deliverance from the evil one. By the grace given you in Baptism, continue in His Word. Daily confess your sin and your slavery to it. By the merciful power of God's Spirit, continue in the Word, daily trusting Jesus for full pardon. Through faithful use of the written Word and regular dining at the Lord's Table, Jesus loosens sin's enslaving grip on your life and sets you free. By Christ's power, you will have the last word over sin: victory!

This is our Reformation heritage. Here is Christ's teaching, emphasized by Martin Luther: repentance and faith are not once-in-a-while actions, but the entire life and attitude of the Christian on earth. Abiding in the saving Word of Jesus throughout our lives is our only hope, for sin's delusion is horrifying, leading to a most unsavory slavery, blinding us to the fact that we are captives of death and hell. To shatter our delusion, to save us slaves, Jesus reveals the truth—the truth of His cross and empty tomb, the truth that sets us free. God's freedom is yours by grace alone, received through faith alone, revealed in Scripture alone. This is the truth that makes you free.

Rev. Charles W. Blanco

November

All Saints' Day

Saints Alive!

Isaiah 35:1–10

"The ransomed of the LORD shall return and come to Zion with singing; everlasting joy shall be upon their heads; they shall obtain gladness and joy, and sorrow and sighing shall flee away" (Is 35:10).

What do we Lutheran Christians do with All Saints' Day? How should we celebrate it? In earlier days the Church emphasized the bold witness of the martyrs, those who gave their lives because they were followers of Jesus Christ. Today, the Church tries to emphasize all saints—those who celebrate life eternal in God's presence in heaven and the followers of Jesus Christ on earth.

So what do we do with All Saints' Day? Surely it's a day to remember with gratitude the lives of those who have gone before us in the faith. Surely it's a day to share the loss of those whose loved ones have passed away. But All Saints' Day is more than that. It's a day to acknowledge two things. First, we all share in the condemnation of the Law. Therefore we die! Second, we all share in the Good News: we are ransomed and redeemed by Christ through His cross. We are the precious possession of God by the blood of Jesus. Therefore we live! All Christians are living saints.

There is a double reason to celebrate the goodness of God today. With those who have lost loved ones to death, we rejoice in this: that parents and children, husbands and wives, friends and strangers, famous people and unknown—all who have died having faith in Jesus Christ—are indeed saints, living saints, in heaven. We remember them with joy and thanksgiving. They already have what Isaiah prophesied in our Scripture reading: "Everlasting joy shall be upon their heads; they shall obtain gladness and joy, and sorrow and sighing shall flee away" (Is 35:10).

But we rejoice also in this: that sainthood is not limited to believers in Christ who have died and gone to be with Christ. Strange as it sounds, you and I, as believers in Christ, are saints too, right here and now—living saints! In the New Testament, the word *saint* is one of the most frequent ways of referring to Christians still living on this earth. The apostle Paul addressed several New Testament letters to God's people in a given place, Ephesus, for example. He wrote this to the people in Ephesus: "To the saints who are in Ephesus, and are faithful in Christ Jesus" (Eph 1:1). To the people in Philippi Paul wrote these words: "To all the saints in Christ Jesus who are at Philippi" (Phil 1:1).

How could Paul do that, you ask. As surely as he knew that *saint* means "holy person," he also knew all about the unholiness and sin in himself and in his fellow Christians. To be called a saint does not mean that we're perfect, that we're always loving and giving, that we never get mad or jealous. We know that it's not true of ourselves, of anyone else here, or even of the best Christians that we know. We're all sinners, condemned under the wrath of God's Law. That's why we die! Paul knew this fact of our human condition to be true of everyone to whom he wrote, that they were sinners headed for the grave. He knew it about himself. He knew it about me. He knew it about you. We all stand as unholy sinners before a perfect, almighty God.

But Paul knew something else about sainthood. He understood that the basis for sainthood is not the ability to pray all day or to be a super volunteer at church or in the community or to be a faithful worshiper all the years of our lives. The only basis for sainthood and for being a forgiven, saved child of God is the sacrifice of Jesus Christ, the Son of God, on the cross of Calvary.

We're saints not because we're sinless, but because our sin has been taken away by God's grace in Jesus Christ. From our Baptism, whether as a baby or an adult, until our death, we're saints in the eyes of God. After our death we continue to be saints, though in far more glorious surroundings. John describes these glorious heavenly surroundings in the Book of Revelation. *(Read Rev 7:9–17.)*

Apply this stunning description of heaven to our current life: No more shaky finances. No more slanderous political campaigns. No more growing worry about our own health, no more anger, no more death. Those who depart in faith have all of this now! It's the gift of Jesus Christ, who came down from heaven to earth, who was born of the Virgin Mary, who sacrificed Himself on the cross of Calvary for our sins once for all time, for all people.

Thank God for the wonderful gift of sainthood He has made a reality for all believers in Jesus. What a wonderful gift, first, that God has called you a saint. Being a saint of God means you are precious to God, bought with a price, the apple of His eye. You are, in Isaiah's words this morning, the "ransomed" and "redeemed" of the Lord. You have been put by God on "the Way of Holiness" Isaiah prophesied (v. 8), fleeing temptation, worshiping in God's house, running from the darkness of sin, fleeing to the light of God's Word. You are living saints, after all!

And if you are a living saint, then so is your fellow Christian. Another person who trusts in Christ is also a saint of God, cleansed by the lifeblood of the Son of God, "redeemed" and "ransomed" by His cross. Think of all those Christians around you made saints by God. Your spouse. Your children. Your classmate. Your colleague at work. All of these people, redeemed by God, brought to faith in Baptism, made into living saints! Praise God for the gift of His Holy Spirit through Jesus Christ, reminding us each day that we are "saints," the "holy ones" of God. Living saints! Alleluia.

Rev. Scott C. Sailer

What Is to Become of Us?

Isaiah 26:1–4, 8–9, 12–13, 19–21

Many people are preoccupied with life after death, usually in one of these three ways: (1) When a loved one dies, it thrusts us into the margins of time and eternity. We wonder what becomes of us. (2) There is an interest in Eastern spirituality, particularly reincarnation. (3) Science and technology have made such quantum leaps in this century that people wonder why the barrier of our mortality cannot be transcended.

For all our discoveries, profound mysteries still remain. How often we are moved to say, "Only God knows." He does reserve certain counsels to Himself. In Holy Writ He reveals enough for us to know that He knows, and He does provide what we need to know to make the transition from this world into the next. We examine these three ways of thinking about life after death on the basis of God's Word through the prophet Isaiah.

Joining the Communion of Saints

There is a universal yearning to know something about the other side. Especially when someone close to us dies, we experience a basic resistance to death because we have a fundamental feeling that we are meant to live, not die, and that we are meant to be related to one another in living, caring relationships.

Since we are people of the Bible, we direct our questions to the Lord God of Israel. "My soul yearns for You in the night," Isaiah prays; "my spirit within me earnestly seeks You" (v. 9). This yearning indicates that we human beings are made to relate to God in a special way. True, our awareness is blurred by sin, but this very yearning is a strong intimation that there is something more for us to become than we are today.

Our reflections are not enough. We need to be assured that God knows, cares, and communicates with us. The Lord's knowing and caring is beautifully expressed in one of the psalms: "As a father shows compassion to his children, so the LORD shows compassion to those who fear Him. For He knows our frame; He remembers that we are dust" (Ps 103:13–14). The psalmist goes on to say that humankind flowers and fades, while God's loving care endures from generation to generation and lasts forever (Ps 103:15–17).

When we think of the faith, the hope, and the love of those followers of Christ who have gone before us, we are directed to the Christ who gave them that life, grace, and hope. In Christ, we are united with those believers who have gone before us. That's why we confess in the Apostles' Creed, "I believe in the communion of saints." A hymn by Isaac Watts and Charles Wesley describes it this way: "The saints on earth and those above But one communion make. . . . Part of the host have passed the flood, And part are crossing now" (*TLH* 478:1, 3). The Common Doxology also could be quoted: "All creatures here below . . . above, ye heav'nly host" (*LSB* 805:1).

In the Order of Holy Communion, worshipers are reminded that they are part of the communion of saints when the pastor invites the congregation to sing the unending hymn of Isaiah 6 with these words: "Therefore with angels and archangels and with all the company of heaven we laud and magnify Your glorious name" (*LSB Altar Book*, p. 161). The congregation intones, "Holy, holy, holy Lord God of pow'r and might: Heaven and earth are full of Your glory. . . . Hosanna in the highest. Blessed is He who comes in the name of the Lord" (*LSB Altar Book*, p. 165).

Our place in the communion of saints rests, however, not in how close we feel to those already in heaven, but on God's gift of grace in Jesus Christ. Because the act is His, the apostle Paul writes, "God's firm foundation stands, bearing this seal: 'The Lord knows those who are His' " (2 Tim 2:19).

Not Reincarnation but Resurrection

The idea of reincarnation means people are supposed to be changed into one form of life after another, to work up from a lower to a better life, depending on their behavior. The process can go on for centuries. The final goal is to be freed from the cycle.

The Scriptures say that Christ died once for all (Heb 7:27; 9:26–28; 10:10). It is not necessary for His death or ours to be repeated. He led the perfect life, sacrificed His life for humankind, and rose again from the dead, to return some day and reclaim us from the dead.

In the chapter before us, Isaiah describes the futility of human efforts to achieve new life or salvation. He uses the metaphor of a pregnancy that does not result in a birth. "We were pregnant, we writhed, but we have given birth to wind. We have accomplished no deliverance in the earth, and the inhabitants of the world have not fallen" (Is 26:18).

But now Isaiah utters one of the most remarkable descriptions of the resurrection of the body to be found in the Hebrew Scriptures. The thought must have come as a flash of light from above: so faithful is God in keeping His promises, so great is God's love and His power! "Your dead shall live; their bodies shall rise." Isaiah is so carried away with prophetic fervor that he addresses the dead: "You who dwell in the dust, awake and sing for joy!" It almost sounds like an Easter anthem. "For your dew is a dew of light, and the earth will give birth to the dead" (Is 26:19).

This prophecy was like a bolt of lightning. At the raising of Lazarus we again hear the thunder of a power greater than death. At the earthquake accompanying Jesus' resurrection we finally feel the full impact of this ancient prophecy. The apostle Paul relates our resurrection so closely to Christ's that he writes, "If there is no resurrection of the dead, then not even Christ has been raised. . . . But in fact Christ has been raised from the dead, the firstfruits of those who have fallen asleep. . . . For as in Adam all die, so also in Christ shall all be made alive" (1 Cor 15:13, 20, 22).

What is to become of us? Not reincarnation but resurrection, restoration, reunion. Something happens that even the prophets and apostles have difficulty describing. " 'What no eye has seen, nor ear heard, nor the heart of man imagined, what God has prepared for those who love Him'—these things God has revealed to us through the Spirit" (1 Cor 2:9–10).

What will happen after death? Scripture gives us glimpses. Some passages suggest that death is like a sleep with a great awakening on resurrection morn. Some passages speak of the angels gathering the elect from the ends of the earth on the Last Day. Some passages liken the resurrection to arriving at the heavenly Jerusalem after a long pilgrimage. Other passages liken it to a beautiful rendition of the "Hallelujah Chorus" or to a banquet feast. Time and space are inverted in a kind of super cosmic cataclysm of joy.

"Now we see in a mirror dimly," the apostle Paul writes, "but then face to face. Now I know in part; then I shall know fully, even as I have been fully known" (1 Cor 13:12). God knows.

When Scripture speaks of the interval of time between now and the day of resurrection, it frequently says it will happen in "a little while" (Is 26:20). Even at the end of the Bible, the Lord says, "Surely I am coming soon" (Rev 22:20).

How long is that "little while," and when is the "soon" complete? It would seem that when we cross over death's threshold, time is no longer a problem. Perhaps from the perspective of eternity it will seem that our death and Christ's return are very close indeed.

We believe not in a series of reincarnations, but in a once-for-all resurrection at the end of time as we know it. Generations ago British Archbishop William Temple put it like this: "I know less about heaven and the hereafter than I do about almost anything else, but it is something I am more sure of than anything else."

WE UNDERGO A METAMORPHOSIS

When we think of all the advances in science and technology, we wonder if any of them might eventually enable us to see through the gateway of death. We're fascinated by reports of what people call near-death or out-of-body experiences. We wish we knew more of Paul's vision in which he was caught up into the third heaven (whatever that is). "Whether in the body or out of the body I do not know," he wrote; "God knows." And he was even caught up to paradise, "Whether in the body or out of the body I do not know, God knows—and He heard things that cannot be told, which man may not utter" (2 Cor 12:2–4).

Paul's experience was unique, personal, and individual, like that of Lazarus, who was raised from the dead and then had to die again. We do not expect those kinds of experiences, but we do know that we, too, will die.

Our bodies will undergo a mighty change (1 Cor 15:52). As a caterpillar has to undergo a metamorphosis to become a butterfly, so we will be changed to live in a new heaven and a new earth. Instead of having angelic wings, the Scriptures tells us we will be like Christ, whom the apostles could touch and feel and who even ate with them after His resurrection.

Meanwhile, our lives are hidden with Christ in God. "When Christ who is your life appears, then you also will appear with Him in glory" (Col 3:4). This definitely will transcend any experiences people might have this side of glory. And it will come about when the Lord returns. "Behold, the LORD is coming" (Is 26:21). Then we shall certainly see what we shall become. As Martin Luther and others have pointed out, my believing and dying are things I do alone as I face my Maker. In this connection, I think there are things we can learn from the elderly, many of whom have learned what lasts and where faith needs to rest. Let me tell you about a 90-year-old gentleman and how he faced the decline of his mental powers. Realizing what was happening, he copied the following poem and slipped it into his Bible so that he could linger over each line and remind himself of God's eternal care. *(The preacher should read the poem "But God" by Annie Johnson Flint in a deliberate style. The poem is available at http://preceptaustin.org/annie's_poems.htm or in* But God *by V. Raymond Edman [Grand Rapids: Zondervan, 1980].)*

God knows. In Christ we are safe. Isn't that enough?

Rev. Paul E. Schuessler

Commemoration of the Faithful Departed

Saints Now and Forever

John 5:24–29

On or about November 1 every year, the Church throughout the world has, from ancient times, celebrated All Saints' Day. It has been a common practice on that day to remember not only the great saints but also those of lesser fame who have died in the faith: someone's grandmother, father, sister, friend, or child. The November 2 festival of the Commemoration of the Faithful Departed developed with just this difference in mind; While individual circumstances and gifts may differ, the faith that saves is the same in every Christian's heart. All believers are saints—living now and forever.

ALL BELIEVERS ARE SAINTS—LIVING ALREADY NOW

One All Saints' Day I had prepared name tags for everyone coming to church. On each tag I had written "Saint." Each person was then to fill in his or her first name so that it read "Saint Ellen," "Saint Robert," and so on. One woman did not write her name on her tag. She told me she didn't feel worthy enough to call herself "saint." This reveals our reluctance to believe the comforting and joyous promise of our Lord, who came to deliver us from death to life, to rescue us and set us apart as His holy ones, His saints, even as we still struggle in this world. According to Jesus' words, death and life refer to more than just physical existence. Death is separation right now from God by unbelief and fear of judgment. Life, on the other hand, is reconciliation today with God by faith in His Son, the comfort of knowing that He endured the judgment against our sin on the cross, and the hope in His power and authority to raise us on the Last Day to life everlasting.

ALREADY NOW THE SPIRITUALLY DEAD HEAR HIS VOICE

The words of Jesus in today's text were spoken precisely to unbelieving hearts who wondered and were even offended by His claim to be who He truly is: the Son of God sent by the Father to deliver all people from the punishment and death of sin. He says that "an hour is coming, and is now here, when the dead will hear the voice of the Son of God" (v. 25). "The dead" means you and me and all who are born into this world with the inherited disease called sin.

Already now, the Son's "judgment" is that we have life

In the beginning God created everything out of nothing, by the power of His Word alone (Gen 1; Heb 11:3). John began his Gospel by identifying Jesus as "the Word" (Jn 1:1). In this text Jesus clearly claims to be the Son of God—God, the Second Person of the Holy Trinity, come in the flesh. Because of this, "as the Father has life in Himself, so He has granted the Son also to have life in Himself. And He has given Him authority to execute judgment" (vv. 26–27).

The Son's judgment is based on the fact that "God so loved the world" (Jn 3:16). But because of the slavery of sin no one can free or save himself. God's love, then, was shown in this, that He sent His only-begotten Son. He was sent by the Father to fulfill perfectly God's righteous demands on our behalf. He came to be the one and only perfect sacrifice for the sin of the whole world, satisfying God's wrath against all sin. His bloody death on the cross was death's undoing as His resurrection from the grave proves. So now His judgment of us is the same as that spoken through the prophet Jeremiah, "I know the plans I have for you, declares the LORD, plans for wholeness and not for evil" (Jer 29:11). For as the apostle Paul said, "He Himself is our peace" (Eph 2:14).

Already now, all who have faith are saints— even as they are still very much alive

Because He is the Son of God, the crucified and risen Savior, "whoever hears My word and believes Him who sent Me has eternal life" (v. 24). For His Word is all about the forgiveness of your sins on the basis of His atoning death for you. Forgiveness means we are now holy, that is, saints!—for being holy, clean of sin, is what it means to be a saint. And where there is forgiveness of sins there also is life and salvation—a present possession. This is what Jesus means when He says "an hour is coming, and is now here" (v. 25). In Christ the separation is ended, the breach is healed. By faith a person has crossed over from death to life. This happens now by the simple hearing of His Word, through which the Holy Spirit creates saving faith in the heart.

All Believers Are Saints— Also in the Resurrection

But that's not all, "for an hour is coming when all who are in the tombs will hear His voice and come out" (vv. 28–29). That time is not yet. Nevertheless, this is the great hope of the Christian faith.

The resurrection at Christ's return is the basis for our Christian comfort

We anticipate that day when the Son of Man returns "with power and great glory" with His angels and a loud trumpet call (Mt 24:30–31), "and the dead in Christ will rise . . . and so we [also] will always be with the Lord" (1 Thess 4:13–18). In that day, says the Lord, "those who have done good," that is, who have believed and lived by faith in His Word, will rise "to the resurrection of life." But "those who have done evil," that is, who have rejected His Word and relied only on their own self-chosen works of unbelief, will rise "to the resurrection of judgment" (v. 29). This is the hope by which, alone, the apostle can tell us to comfort one another at the death of a loved one or in facing the hour of our own death.

In the comfort of the resurrection, we saints can depart in peace

Remember the story of Simeon, to whom it was revealed "that he would not see death before he had seen the Lord's Christ" (Lk 2:26). When Mary and Joseph brought the infant Jesus to the temple, Simeon took Him in his arms and praised God, saying, "Lord, now you are letting your servant depart in peace, according to your word" (Lk 2:29). This canticle has found a beloved place in the liturgy after we have taken our Savior (or, better, He has given Himself) not into our arms, but sacramentally into our mouths in Holy Communion. That peace is none other than the peace of the forgiveness of sins won for us by the shedding of Christ's blood. Our "departing in peace" from each celebration of the Sacrament prepares us for our final departure from death to life through forgiveness and the strengthening of faith. "For as often as you eat this bread and drink the cup, you proclaim the Lord's death until He comes" (1 Cor 11:26). Our hope is "in the cross of our Lord Jesus Christ, by which the world has been crucified to me, and I to the world" (Gal 6:14).

When we hear the words of David in today's psalm, "I sought the LORD, and He answered me and delivered me from all my fears. . . . Fear the LORD, you His saints, for those who fear Him have no lack" (Ps 34:4, 9), we may be tempted to think he had to be a giant pillar of faith to speak those words. But David spoke those words because he needed to hear them. For it is by the Word of God alone that faith is given and strengthened and that hope endures, even in the face of death and everything that speaks against it. Today, as we remember those who have gone before us with the sign of faith—both the more famous and the more personal saints—we comfort one another with the fact that they are with the Lord. And we rejoice that, having heard the Lord's Word, we "know You the only true God, and Jesus Christ whom You have sent" (Jn 17:3), and "that by believing you may have life in His name" (Jn 20:31). To you, His saints—set apart from sin for His worship and service—He says again today, "Depart in peace."

Rev. Allen D. Lunneberg

St. Andrew, Apostle

Introducing Peter's Brother

Matthew 4:18–22

Have you ever been introduced as the brother, son, or wife of someone? The introducer wants to connect you with someone who is better known than you are. It almost seems as if you aren't your own person, as if your real identity is tied up in someone else. You feel like a nonperson.

I am sure that many times Andrew the apostle was introduced as Peter's brother, though he was the one who brought Peter and introduced him to Jesus in the first place. Peter was loud, outspoken, and boisterous. He was the kind of person you knew was there. I am sure he was often the first of the disciples to be noticed when they went somewhere together. The Scriptures tell us a lot about Peter. They even include two of his letters. On the other hand, we hear little about Peter's brother, Andrew.

Despite his lack of recognition, there is much we learn from the apostle Andrew. The Church has set aside November 30 to recognize this great man of God. As we search the Scriptures, we quickly learn that he was a fisherman who took seriously his call to become a fisher of men.

A Fisherman

Robert Morley, in *Pardon Me, But You're Eating My Doily!* tells about an embarrassing event in the life of Sidney Sheldon. A few days after he acquired a lovely blue Rolls-Royce, Sheldon parked in front of a shop in Beverly Hills. After concluding his shopping, he got in the car. An arm reached through the window, grabbed his shoulder, and said, "What do you think you're doing?" He looked up and saw an enormous Texan, who said, "This is my car."

"No, it isn't," Sheldon insisted. "It's mine." To prove it, he put the key to the ignition. But it didn't fit. Then he realized what had happened. He said, "I'm terribly sorry, but I'm driving the same model and color Rolls as you, and obviously I parked right in back of you." As the huge stranger watched, Sheldon got out of the car and walked back to his wife's white Volkswagen, which he was driving that morning.[8]

---

8 Robert Morley, *Pardon Me, But You're Eating My Doily!* (New York: St. Martin's Press, 1983).

There are things in life that make us feel pretty small and insignificant. In fact, there are times when we feel totally out of place. We've said the wrong thing, done the wrong thing at the wrong time, and watched our Rolls-Royce shrink to a Volkswagen as we found ourselves feeling totally inadequate for a job. Many of us have felt that way when called upon to do certain tasks. "I just can't do that," we responded.

In today's text we encounter Jesus walking by the Sea of Galilee, passing two fishermen, Peter and Andrew, and saying to them, "Follow Me, and I will make you fishers of men" (Mt 4:19). These two have spent their lives fishing. They are not scholars or men with powerful influence. They have no great background and certainly no great future. They are just simple working people. With no hesitation, Jesus chooses these men to be His disciples, His students.

This was probably not the first encounter these two brothers had with Jesus. John the Baptist had introduced Andrew to Jesus, calling Jesus the Lamb of God. Andrew, in turn, ran to get His brother and introduced Him to Jesus (Jn 1:35–42). Now, all of a sudden, Jesus chose both of them to be His disciples.

As we walk through the pages of Scripture we learn that God loves to work with the "little people," the common, everyday person who holds no high office or rank, the person who has no heritage to flaunt or airs to put on. Jesus comes to common people like you and me and calls us to follow Him. It was on the day of our Baptism, as the water splashed on our heads, that He specifically called to you and me, saying, "I love you. I want you to follow Me." As this call rings in our ears today we learn from Andrew how to continue to respond to His call.

Who Took Seriously His Call

"You're pretty brave coming down in a parachute in a one-hundred-mile-an-hour wind," the farmer said to the soldier. "I didn't come down in a parachute," said the soldier. "I went up in a tent." With that kind of intensity Jesus' call picked up Andrew, and moved him to leave everything behind and immediately follow Jesus. There was no doubt in Andrew's mind. This is what he must do with his life. Now everything else is second to Jesus. Andrew was convinced that Jesus was the promised Messiah, the Savior of the world. It is this conviction that moves him, without any hesitation, to leave behind his possessions and way of life and follow Jesus.

The same wind is blowing at our tent today. The question is, Will it lift us up and move us out into the world, or have we staked it down and weighted it down with our own hopes and dreams, with our own material things, so that the wind of the Spirit has a difficult time moving us?

Andrew looked at Jesus. Christ's person was everything that Andrew needed to make a decision. The same is true for us today. Nothing can motivate us more quickly than to stop and look at Jesus. As we focus on His forgiving eyes, hear His reassuring voice, "You are My sheep and I am your Shepherd," and feel His healing touch on our sin-ridden bodies, we find ourselves, like Andrew, moved to respond to His call with eagerness and with thanksgiving.

Often we ask older adults if they would have done things differently, if they had only known what they do now. Andrew may have quickly answered, "Now I know Jesus." That made a tremendous difference in his life and, to be sure, it makes a tremendous difference in our life. The life, death, and resurrection of Jesus turns our lives upside down. Instead of saying, "Count me out—I don't think I can do it," we find ourselves saying, "Count me in—I am going to follow Jesus!"

To Fish for Men

A salesman was writing an order for five hundred ballpoint pens. He had just convinced a store owner he needed the pens to improve his business. All at once the owner turned and said to the salesman, "Hold everything. I'm canceling my order." With that he turned and began waiting on a customer. The salesman closed his book and angrily left the store. A little later a clerk asked the store owner, "Why did you cancel that order so quickly?" He replied, "He told me how important it was to use ballpoint pens and had me convinced, then he proceeded to write my order with a pencil. He didn't even use his own product!"

As we follow the life of Andrew, there is no doubt that he relied heavily on the person he recommended to others. Andrew was convinced that Jesus Christ was the Savior of the world—and his Savior! Jesus was so important to Andrew that the apostle couldn't keep himself from speaking about Him to others. Each time Andrew is mentioned in the Gospels he is bringing someone to Jesus.

Andrew starts with his own family. After he meets Jesus, the first person he brings to Jesus is his brother (Jn 1:40–42). Andrew becomes a good model for our witnessing. Talking about Jesus starts at home with our families. As we go about our everyday lives, those who are closest to us—those with whom we have the most contact—are the members of our families. We naturally talk with our families about Jesus. Daily we reacquaint family members with their Lord and ours. We invite any who don't know Him to meet Him, so they, too, might experience His love and forgiveness. An invitation to meet Jesus in Bible study, in a church service, or in our own conversation and witness helps our relatives to realize how much Jesus means to us, so like Peter, they will be curious to find out who is making us so excited.

The next time we meet Andrew, he is leading a small boy to Jesus (Jn 6:8–9). Jesus is talking to a crowd of five thousand people and they find themselves in the wilderness at suppertime without food. Andrew, convinced that Jesus can perform miracles, brings to Jesus a little boy with his lunch of five small loaves and two fish. We know the rest of that story. By introducing a boy to Jesus, five thousand people were introduced to Jesus as the bread of life come down from heaven—the one who satisfies their deepest spiritual hunger. God used Andrew to touch a multitude.

There is no end to what God can and will do with our witness. He only asks us to be faithful and bring others to Him. He will then use this witness to accomplish His purpose. Our witness to a child or to a friend may be God's first step in molding that person to do great things in His kingdom in the future.

Finally, we find Andrew with Philip, bringing some inquiring Greeks to meet Jesus. Andrew's witness was not limited to the Jews. He was ready, willing, and eager to cross cultures and bring to Jesus anyone who would listen. Not only was he the first home missionary, he was also the first foreign missionary. Tradition tells us that after Pentecost Andrew took the Gospel to India and spent the rest of his life proclaiming the Good News.

Today as we see God reversing the mission fields by bringing the fields to us, we are faced with a similar challenge. Are we ready to communicate the Good News of Jesus Christ cross-culturally? Are we ready to find ways to bring all the diverse cultures in our midst to meet Jesus? Are we, like Andrew, despite their color, language, or culture, ready to say, "Come, I will take you to meet Jesus"? In our United States of America, God has reversed the escalator. Now, instead of us sending a few missionaries over to foreign lands to introduce them to Jesus Christ, God is bringing multitudes of people from around the world to our doorsteps so we can more easily say to them, "Come, I would like for you to meet Jesus."

We may not hear a lot about Andrew, but it is quite obvious that after meeting Jesus, he did not feel or act like a nonperson. He knew Jesus Christ as his Savior, and he was anxious that everyone with whom he came in contact would also get to know Jesus. God used him to accomplish great things in His kingdom. Today, as we once again recognize this great apostle of our Lord, it helps us to understand a little more clearly that regardless of who we are or how small or ineffective we might feel in our congregation, by the splash of our Baptism God has called us to be His disciples, and He is daily using us to touch the lives of people as we talk to others about this Jesus, who means so much to us. No longer are we nonpersons. We are called to be disciples of Jesus. As we follow Him He will use us to accomplish great things in His kingdom.

Rev. Kenneth W. Behnken

December

St. Thomas, Apostle

The Last Picture of the Twin

Acts 1:12–14

By the last week before Christmas, almost all of the Christmas cards for this year have arrived, complete with notes and letters. Many families send photos so that each year those who receive them can see how the family has changed—how the children have grown or how they have all matured. These annual portraits often include "first pictures" of newborn babies and people who marry into the clan. They may also contain "last pictures" of people who have died or have left the family circle for some reason. In our text today we have the "last picture" of St. Thomas given us in the Scriptures.

The portrait in words that St. Luke paints for us in the first chapter of Acts is that of a very special group. It includes the eleven disciples, the women who followed Jesus (including Mary, His mother), and the brothers of Jesus. Thomas is part of the group in that upper room, part of the faithful who are together constantly in prayer. Thomas is in the picture. There is a place for him among the faithful. And there is a place for each of us as well.

Thomas generally does not get much good press in Scripture. The few times that he is described individually, he appears in a less than flattering light. He seems both skeptical and impulsive. He asks questions when he should know the answers. Martin Luther talks about the "carnal manner" of Thomas, who wants to know the earthly road Jesus is traveling, missing entirely the heavenly destination to which He was going (Jn 14:5). Even at his best moments in the Gospels, Thomas seems to come up short, suggesting that going with Jesus to the grave of Lazarus would certainly bring death, not only to the master but also to all His disciples (Jn 11:16). We know him as "doubting Thomas," the name he earned by wanting to touch the risen Jesus in person before he would believe in the resurrection (Jn 20:25). In his own way, Thomas is a disciple for us and for our times.

We, too, are people frequently more doubtful than devoted. We, too, find ourselves questioning and uncertain. We, too, have things about our personalities and lives that can lead us to doubt our presence in the picture of God's faithful people. Remembering things we have said and done in the past, we, too, may come to the conclusion that we should be excluded when the saints get together in the eternal Upper Room that Jesus has prepared. We know our sins and our shortcomings, even if they are well concealed from others—and, more important, God knows them. He knows what we really are like. How can He love and accept us? In this Advent season of hope, is there hope that we are part of God's picture?

The last picture of the twin says it all: there is room for Thomas among the disciples. Despite his doubting and his questioning and all of his other character flaws, he is among the faithful. By the grace of God, Thomas finally knew and believed that Jesus is the Messiah, who died and rose again for his sins. The doubting disciple found forgiveness, acceptance, and hope. The last picture of Thomas encourages us as we realize that we are in the same picture.

There is room among the faithful for those who at times are doubters and questioners as they reflect carefully and frequently on what they believe and why. Despite Thomas' unwillingness to believe the disciples' first report of the resurrected Jesus, on the evening of that first day of the week, Jesus makes a second appearance. He comes back again. And Thomas, through this encounter, is led to confess, "My Lord and my God!" (Jn 20:28). He exclaims in a single sentence the truth of who Jesus is: God incarnate, crucified for our sins, and risen from the grave. Thomas's doubting becomes a lesson for us. Doubt is a form of unbelief and therefore is sinful. But as we find forgiveness and assurance in Jesus Christ, our doubts can be short-lived, as the writer of our sermon hymn writes:

> All praise, O Lord, for Thomas
> Whose short-lived doubtings prove
> Your perfect twofold nature,
> The fullness of Your love.
> To all who wait with questions
> A steadfast faith afford;
> And grant us grace to know You,
> True man, yet God and Lord. (*LSB* 517:6)

So there is a positive side to doubting Thomas. Actually, he has a number of strengths. He has a searching mind and a valiant heart. He is ready to be a martyr for Jesus, ready to put his life on the line for his Savior. His day on the church calendar is the last saint's day before Christmas. Tradition tells us that Thomas indeed did become a martyr, that he became the apostle to India, that he proclaimed the Gospel and established churches there, and that finally he was put to death with a spear at the order of one of the local rulers. Many believers in India still refer to themselves as "St. Thomas Christians."

What a wonderful legacy to leave behind! There is room in the picture of the faithful for heroes and heroines in all generations of the Church. Thomas is the last saint before Christmas; Stephen is the first saint after the celebration. Both were martyrs. Each was faithful in both life and death. Their presence on the calendar at this joyful, hopeful time of Jesus' birth helps us see the cost of faith. "Let us also go," Thomas says to the other disciples, "that we may die with Him" (Jn

11:16). Thomas did die, not with but for the Lord. The spear on his traditional shield tells the story.

Of course, the spear is not the only item on the shield of St. Thomas. There is a carpenter's square as well. Tradition says he built a church with his own hands. Certainly his witness as an apostle did build churches wherever he went. Whether or not he had skill as a carpenter, he could build for the glory of God. There is a need for builders in Christ's picture of the Church. And there is a place for whatever talents and abilities you have to use in the service of your Lord—that Lord Jesus Christ, who loves you and gave His life for you. Each of you is very special to Him—special as an individual. Just like Thomas, the twin. Which raises an interesting question: whose twin was Thomas?

In the lists of the apostles in Scripture, Thomas is paired with Matthew (who was also called Levi and was a son of Alphaeus, Mk 2:14), and he is listed before James, who is specifically called the son of Alphaeus (Mk 3:18). So the suggestion is that Thomas is Matthew's twin, and that all three—Thomas, Matthew, and James—were brothers. Perhaps that is true. But it really doesn't matter. What matters is not Thomas's relationship to the other disciples, but his relationship to the Lord. The same is true of you and me.

Perhaps you have received all sorts of greetings from lots of friends and relatives during this Christmas season. Perhaps you are related to other people in this congregation, perhaps not. What matters is that you are a part of the big picture, the group portrait of those who live by faith in the Lord. The picture from our text for today shows us a great variety of people. What brings them together and makes them one is the faith they share—a living and growing faith in the resurrected Lord Jesus Christ. "All these with one accord were devoting themselves to prayer," St. Luke tells us (Acts 1:14). They prayed together and then went out to serve their Lord—just as we are called to do.

It is fitting that we observe the day of St. Thomas as we bring this year's Advent season toward its close. It is a way to remind us that the baby of Bethlehem is the Lord with wounds in His hands and side, that He is the risen one who is our Lord and God. It is a day for us to see a person who, despite all his human failings, used his gifts and abilities to the glory of God, one who puts his hope into action. It is a day for us to honor the twin, for in so doing we follow the Lutheran directive found in the Apology of the Augsburg Confession, which states, "Our Confession approves honoring the saints in three ways. The first is thanksgiving. We should thank God because He has shown examples of mercy, because He wishes to save people, and because He has given teachers and other gifts to the Church. . . . The second service is the strengthening of our faith. . . . We also are encouraged to believe all the more that grace truly superabounds over sin (Romans 5:20). The third honor is the imitation, first of faith, then of the other virtues. Everyone should imitate the saints according to his calling" (Apology of the Augsburg Confession XXI 4–6; *Concordia*, p. 202).

The last picture of the twin is a picture of faith and hope. As we travel in heart and mind to Bethlehem in the coming days, we will experience again the wonder of God coming to our fallen world in the person of His Son. May we be renewed in both faith and in hope, rejoicing that each of us, by God's grace, has a place in God's picture and in the eternal kingdom of Christ.

Rev. Gregory Wismar

St. Stephen's Day

God Is with Us

Acts 6:8–7:2a, 51–60

If I were to ask you to describe the message of Christmas in just one word, what word would you choose? You probably could find no better word than *Immanuel*. Immanuel is the name God ascribed through the prophet Isaiah to the infant who would be born of the virgin. It means "God is with us."

Isn't this the message of Christmas: that in Christ, God is with us? Isn't this the miracle of miracles: that the Word, who was with the Father from eternity, became flesh and dwelt among us? Now ascended to His glorious throne in heaven, He is with us still to lead, help, and comfort us. This is the message we confess to our world and in which we ourselves find comfort: God is with us.

Today (December 26) is the day that the Church has chosen to remember her first martyr after Christ, St. Stephen. To some the day after Christmas may seem an odd day to speak of such a dreary subject as persecution and martyrdom. But when we keep in mind the Christmas message, God is with us, we see that this topic may have timely value after all. The martyrdom of Stephen allows us to explore more deeply what it means to have God with us.

SOMETIMES IT IS DIFFICULT TO SEE THAT GOD IS WITH US

In a world like ours, it is sometimes difficult to see that God is with us. While Yugoslavia was under Communist rule, a Christian man was imprisoned and tortured. Eventually, his hope and courage changed to despair. He hanged himself and left the following note for his wife: "I have gone to remind God of a world he has forgotten."[9] Don't people often ask, "If there is a God, why all the suffering?" Why do bad things so often happen to relatively good people? Where is God when a baby is aborted, a child abused, an older person neglected? Where is God as ungodliness grows around us?

Surely the Christians in Stephen's day wondered the same thing. Here was one of their brothers whom they greatly admired. He was "a man full of faith and of the Holy Spirit" (Acts 6:5). He was a man whom God had blessed with wonderful gifts. They had chosen him as a deacon to help with the distribution of food in the

---

9   Richard Wurmbrand, *Reaching toward the Heights* (Grand Rapids: Zondervan, 1977).

church. They found Stephen to be a courageous man too. Out of love for his Savior, he boldly confessed Jesus as the Christ in the Jewish synagogue.

That's when the conflict arose. Some of the learned rabbis from the synagogue began to argue with Stephen, trying to refute his teachings about the Christ. But God was with Stephen, so these opponents "could not withstand the wisdom and the Spirit with which he was speaking" (Acts 6:10). So far, so good. But then things really began to get ugly. Unable to refute his teaching, his opponents began a smear campaign against him. They bribed some men to tell lies about him and his teaching. Then they arrested him and tried him for blasphemy. But Stephen was sure that God was with him, so he continued courageously in his confession of God's Word. This increased the anger and hatred of his enemies. Finally they could stand it no longer. "They cried out with a loud voice and stopped their ears and rushed together at him. Then they cast him out of the city and stoned him" (7:57–58). The Church might well have wondered, "Where is God in all of this?"

The martyrdom of Stephen reminds us of something we need to remember: this world is a fallen world. It is a world in which our adversary, the devil, still prowls around like a roaring lion, seeking to frighten and devour us. So even though Christmas teaches us that God is with us, we must expect many trials and heartaches in this world.

The account of Stephen takes us even further. It teaches us that many of our conflicts come as a direct result of confessing Christ and His Word. If Stephen had kept his faith to himself, or at least kept it inside the small circle of believers, he could have avoided conflict. But he loved his Savior and his countrymen too much to let them perish in unbelief. It was Stephen's public confession of Christ that led to his death.

In the same way, our confession of Christ and His Word can lead to conflict. Although none of us has yet experienced persecution to the extent that Stephen did, many of us have died "little deaths" for the sake of Christ. Perhaps it came in the form of conflict between a parent and a child, one of whom departed from the faith; or a smear campaign against us or our church by those who think our faith is too rigid or outdated. Perhaps it came in the form of mockery from colleagues at work or an icy stare from the man at the door as we canvass for our church. The story of Stephen reminds us how true this is: the more boldly we confess our faith, the more likely we are to suffer conflict with our world. Surely, all of us have felt the pressure just to keep our faith to ourselves. To counter that pressure in a world like ours, we need the assurance that God is with us.

Christ Assures Us That God Is with Us

The narrative of Stephen gives us that assurance. Notice what Stephen did in the darkest hour of his persecution. "He, full of the Holy Spirit, gazed into heaven and saw the glory of God, and Jesus standing at the right hand of God" (Acts 7:55). It is in Christ that Stephen found the assurance that God was with him, despite his enemies and their threats. This same Christ, whom Stephen believed and confessed, had given up the riches of heaven, had come to earth, and was born in a manger. This Christ, whom Stephen saw enthroned in heaven, is the same one who had suffered and died as the sacrifice for Stephen's sins. The Savior who had paid such a great price for Stephen's salvation would never desert him in his hour of need. Seeing Christ gave Stephen assurance that God was with him.

Do we have that same assurance? We have not seen Christ visibly in the way that Stephen did. But we have seen Him just as certainly in His Word and Sacraments. Every time we read our Bible or devotion book or listen to a sermon, we see Christ and His love for us. We see how much He sacrificed for our salvation, and we are assured again that He will never leave us or forsake us. Every time we come to the Lord's Table, we receive the very body and blood that Christ gave for the forgiveness of sins, and we are assured again of our Lord's commitment to us even in our dark times.

In this world we endure trials and troubles. Sometimes we suffer severely. But as we look to our Savior, we see one who knows what it is to suffer. We see the one who once cried out to His Father, "My God, My God, why have You forsaken Me?" Because Jesus was forsaken by His Father as He bore our sin for us, we know that we never will be left alone. As we gaze intently upon our Savior, God demonstrates to us that He is with us—even in our worst suffering.

God Is with Us, Giving Us Courage to Confess Christ

God's gracious presence with us also gives us courage to confess our Savior and His Word to others. We marvel at the courage of Stephen to stand up before these dangerous men. In the face of death, he never wavered in his confession of Christ.

Does it make you a little ashamed to think of times you chose the easy way out in the face of lesser dangers? It is not easy to be bold confessors of the Savior. Where do we find courage like Stephen's? We find it in Jesus' promise to be with us. Hasn't He promised to be with us as we confess Him? Hasn't He promised to give us the strength to do so? After Jesus commissioned His Church to "go therefore and make disciples of all nations" (Mt 28:19), He added the promise, "Behold, I am with you always, to the end of the age" (v. 20). Before our Lord left this world, He promised His followers that He would not leave them as orphans, but would send the Holy Spirit to help them testify about Him (Jn 15:26–27).

Richard Wurmbrand, a Romanian pastor, tells of being imprisoned with another Christian who had been tortured terribly. When he and other prisoners would fret over their sorrows, this prisoner would say to them, "If the outlook is bad, try the uplook."[10] Then he would remind them of how Stephen, when he was surrounded by hostile men who were about to stone him, looked up to Christ for courage. It is in the "uplook" that we also find courage, even when the outlook seems bad. Knowing God is with us, we find courage to walk in the way of our Savior.

God Is with Us, Assuring Us That He Works All Things Together for Good

We find courage because we know that the God who is with us works all things together for our good (Rom 8:28). The "good" here means especially the salvation of souls and the glory of God.

This good is seen in the martyrdom of Stephen. After his death, intense persecution scattered the members of the Jerusalem church. Many fled Jerusalem and went to the regions of Judea and Samaria. But God used this scattering to accomplish His plan. In fact, the Greek root verb for this scattering (Acts 8:1, 4) is also used for the sowing of seed. God had told His disciples that they would "be [His] witnesses in Jerusalem and in all Judea and Samaria, and to the end of the earth" (Acts 1:8). Persecution was the tool God used to enable them to do that. The Christians established churches wherever they went and, inspired by Stephen's witness, they boldly proclaimed the Gospel.

How many thousands of souls were saved as a result of this? Only God knows. Think of the impact that Stephen's courageous confession must have had even on the enemies of the Gospel. Think of how his prayer for their forgiveness must have pierced their hearts. Could his faithfulness to Christ have made a lasting impression on some of those enemies?

One of those who participated in the death of Stephen and witnessed his courage that day was the Pharisee Saul, who would one day become the apostle Paul, the courageous confessor of Christ.

God can also use our faithfulness to Christ to make an impact on others and bring honor to His name. Think, for instance, of the impact that a father's example of faithfulness to Christ and His Word might have on His children. Think of how, when we forgive our enemies, our action speaks to them about the love and forgiveness we have received from our Savior. Yes, God uses our humble faithfulness to bring honor to His name.

This account of Stephen gives us the comforting assurance that God is with us. May it also give us the courage to stand up for our Savior, who stood up for us on the cross and now stands ready to give us the crown of everlasting life. Amen.

Rev. Stephen F. Gallo

---

10 Wurmbrand, *Reaching toward the Heights.*

St. John, Apostle and Evangelist

Hold the Baby

1 John 1:1–2:2

Most of us find it very easy to warm up to Christmas. The season is so soft and warm and fuzzy. It's friendly and cordial, full of good will. After all, a baby is at the center of the holiday, and who can resist a baby? Christmas is all about the birth of the baby Jesus.

And don't we all love babies? A newborn baby can bring great joy and excitement. Babies can bring out the best in us. Automatically we may respond to them. We want to reach out and embrace them. We want to hug and to hold them. St. John seems to express this same sentiment in 1 John 1. Of course, he writes with more exalted language and with the memory of an exalted Christ. Still, with the baby Jesus in mind, John's words take on even more poignant meaning.

"That which was from the beginning, which we have heard, which we have seen with our eyes, which we looked upon and have touched with our hands, concerning the word of life" (1 Jn 1:1). The arrival, the appearance of this Word of life, can't be stated more clearly. We've listened to the baby. Who hasn't heard a baby coo and cry? We've seen the baby with our eyes of faith. We've looked at Him and touched Him. "The Word became flesh" (Jn 1:14)—right before our eyes! Christmas means that Christ, the very Son of God, comes to us as an infant. This is our theme: hold the baby, for our God comes to us in human form. This point is stressed in a statement supposedly made by Martin Luther: "We cannot draw Christ too deeply into the flesh."

THE CHRIST-BABY ACCEPTS US

You know you don't have to work to win acceptance from babies. Automatically, they accept you. Their approval doesn't depend on your good looks, your education, your proper manners, your politically correct words, or your speaking with the right accent. Babies couldn't care less about the car you drive, the perfume you wear, or the style of clothes you put on. Babies accept you as you are.

Now I ask you: if babies accept you as you are, how much more will the baby Jesus? How much more will your loving, heavenly Father, your Creator and the Creator of all babies? You don't have to earn a baby's approval any more than you have to earn God's approval. God gives love freely, simply because God wants to give love and because God wants to love you.

Lurid misdeeds in your life don't matter to a baby. Past hurts may persist in torturing you, but they don't matter to a baby. The loads of guilt and shame we may carry, they just don't matter to a baby. If you're staggering today under the weight of a bundle of sins, feel free to throw it away. In its place, pick up the Christ-baby. Hold Him in your arms. He loves you. He accepts you as you are. That's our Lord; that's your baby Jesus.

THE CHRIST-BABY MAKES AN IMPACT ON US BY HIS SHEER PRESENCE

His name, Immanuel, tells it all. *Immanuel*—God with us. He lives and stays with us. His abiding presence is all. Just being here presents an all-powerful witness. When you think of it, the presence of babies is about all they have to offer. Babies don't work; they don't produce a thing; they never bring home a salary; they never make a profit; they never make the bed. Since they're here, all we can do is to look at them. You've caught yourself doing it again and again. You stand there by the crib and just stare at this wondrous miracle. You feel enthralled, captivated just because they're here. We may find it difficult to comprehend, but it's true: being is as important as doing.

When I call on people in the hospital, I say a prayer for the medicine to work effectively. I pray that doctors and nurses will make right medical decisions. I pray that surgeons will be skillful. Before I leave, I pray that patients will become conscious of the presence of the Lord Christ because, underneath, His everlasting arms are supporting them. Hovering over them, His everlasting wings protect them. Jesus is here; He's ever-present, and just His being here carries such power for reassurance and healing.

If a cross hangs on the wall, it reminds them that their Suffering Savior is present. He's suffering too. He has suffered for them. He's now suffering for them. If patients receive Holy Communion, they "see with their eyes" and touch and taste our Lord, who is present right here in the Sacrament. Take and hold the body of Christ. Take and eat. Take, drink. The baby is here. Contemplate and celebrate His presence.

THE CHRIST-BABY BRINGS COMFORT AND STRENGTH

Now I'd like to share with you something very personal. I'm not sure I can explain it because I don't really understand it. But you may identify with it anyway. When I've faced trouble in my life, grieved over some loss, struggled to resolve a conflict, or despaired over a failure, I was tempted to give up. At that moment, I used to gather up in my arms the youngest and smallest of our four children. And I held her close. I hugged her tenderly, as though she were a fragile infant, which she was.

This little child could not solve my problems or take my troubles away. She could not wave her tiny hand like a wand and magically turn my failures into successes. She was utterly helpless. But somehow, in a way I can't understand, she gave me the comfort and strength I needed to carry on. Holding her, I could not give up.

When our Lord came into the flesh, He gave up all His power and took on our helplessness. He became as helpless as a tiny baby. From the depths, from desperation and despair, look to the Christ-baby and cradle Him in your arms. Hold Him close. He will comfort you and strengthen you. He will help you cope with all of life's ups and downs and pains and uncertainties.

Visit a nursing home and watch old folks sitting there, holding a baby. They're smiling. "He loves me," the older one says, "and I love him too." So does our Lord. Imitate the aging Simeon who went into the temple in Jerusalem. He took the Christ-baby in his arms and said, "Lord, now You are letting Your servant depart in peace, according to Your word; for my eyes have seen Your salvation" (Lk 2:29–30). Hold the Christ-baby and see your salvation.

You carpenters with your rough and calloused hands, gently pick up your baby and hold Him close. I'd like to think that Joseph did exactly that. All of you Josephs and Marys everywhere, listen to the Christ-baby. Look at Him, and with your hands reach out and touch Him. This little one, this Word of Life, accepts you as you are, promises to be with you always, and brings you comfort and strength.

Rev. Karl Schuessler

St. John—
Apostle, Evangelist, Friend

John 21:7

"On the third day of Christmas my true love sent to me three French hens," or so the well-known holiday song suggests. Each of the days of Christmas has something special happening on it—all the way to Epiphany. That is true for us in the Church as well as for the person in the song, who has a house filled with drummers drumming, ladies dancing, and partridges in pear trees. On the calendar of the Church, the days following the celebration of the Lord's birth are given over to special observances, including the day of St. John, which we now observe.

A strong tradition in church history suggests that John was Jesus' cousin—that John's mother, Salome, and Jesus' mother, Mary, were sisters (both being daughters of Joachim and Anna of Jerusalem). John was part of the inner circle of the disciples, along with Peter and James. Most important, however, is the strong witness of John: the witness to Jesus as the Word made flesh, God with us in person. On this third day of Christmas, then, we faithfully observe the day of St. John—apostle, evangelist, and friend of Jesus—finding in him an example and an encouragement to each of us.

An apostle is one who is sent out on a mission. A number of times during His years of ministry with the disciples, Jesus sent them out to teach and to heal in His name. By those experiences, Jesus was training them to be not just disciples—people who listen to their teacher and take in His message—but apostles, those who are sent out to proclaim their teacher's message and put it into action.

In the Book of Acts, we have a number of portraits of John as an apostle. In Acts 4, we see him and Peter in Jerusalem before the rulers, elders, and teachers of the law. St. Luke tells us that they both were "teaching the people and proclaiming in Jesus the resurrection from the dead" (Acts 4:2). When forbidden to do this, they responded, "We cannot but speak of what we have seen and heard" (v. 20). And they kept on speaking and speaking. Later in the Book of Acts we find John and Peter traveling to Samaria to share in the excitement of the Holy Spirit at work there (8:14–25).

Church tradition finds John as an apostle at a number of places throughout his life. His later years place him in exile on Patmos, an island in the Aegean Sea; finally, he comes to the end of his life in Ephesus, one of the major cities of the ancient world. Wherever he went, John was an apostle, a faithful witness to and worker for the Lord.

By our Baptism, we, too, are called to be faithful witnesses and workers for our Lord. We know the blessed work to which we are summoned. But so often we find ourselves not living up to our baptismal calling. Either we go off in the wrong direction, or we don't do anything at all in response to the Lord's presence in our lives.

John was the same way. At one point (Lk 9:54), we read of his misguided zeal in wanting to call down fire on villages that did not welcome Jesus. We sense his competitiveness in the group of disciples as his mother asks special honors for him and his brother James (Mt 20:20–21; cf. Mk 10:35–37). We find ourselves disappointed by his inability to stay awake with Jesus in the Garden of Gethsemane (Mt 26:36–45 and parallels).

John is not always a great disciple. Yet in the words of John himself, he is a "disciple whom Jesus loved" (Jn 21:7). He experiences the forgiveness that can only be found in Jesus. He repents. He changes. And he grows. Repentance, change, and growth are part of the life of each Christian as we, by grace, live in the forgiveness of sins that Jesus purchased for us by His suffering, death, and resurrection. Maybe it's a good idea that St. John's day comes so close to the beginning of the New Year. Perhaps among our resolutions we can desire, by the power of the Spirit, to live more fully as servants of Jesus—and even as evangelists.

That is the second title given to St. John on this day. He is an apostle and an evangelist—one of those four who put the Gospel into writing and extended its reach in that way. The traditional symbol associated with St. John is the eagle. Some say this is because his words are so lofty that they soar and bring the reader close to heaven itself. All of the writings associated with St. John—his Gospel, his three epistles, and Revelation—have a beauty and divine loftiness to them. John intends that they lift us up and give us assurance of salvation. "I write these things to you who believe in the name of the Son of God that you may know that you have eternal life" (1 Jn 5:13).

Not only did the "little children" (1 Jn 2:1) who received his first letter find encouragement in the words, but nineteen centuries later so also do we. Encouragement is certainly a theme of the Revelation of St. John. In the first part of that singular book of the Bible, he records how he is told by the angel, "Write what you see in a book and send it to the seven churches" (Rev 1:11). And so he does, taking us up for an eagle's eye view of the heavenly city—the New Jerusalem—that is to be our eternal dwelling place. In the hymn "By All Your Saints in Warfare," Horatio Nelson gives thanks for that vision as he writes:

> For Your belov'd disciple
> Exiled to Patmos' shore

And for his faithful record,
We praise You evermore.
Praise for the mystic vision
Through him to us revealed;
May we, in patience waiting,
With Your elect be sealed. (*LSB* 517:8)

Through the pages of his Gospel, John the evangelist helps us to see the glory of the Word made flesh. He includes lofty teachings not shared by the other evangelists—teachings that bring to his readers the good news of the arrival of God's kingdom in Jesus Christ.

Of course John knows his limitations. In today's Gospel we hear him close with the words, "Now there are also many other things that Jesus did. Were every one of them to be written, I suppose that the world itself could not contain the books that would be written" (Jn 21:25).

The fact that he could not share everything, however, did not keep him from sharing something—something very important. And that is an example for us. Sometimes we think that what we want to say or write about our Lord Jesus is not adequate. So we don't say or write anything, thus we miss the opportunity to be evangelists in our time. John knew that he was limited. But that did not stop him from sharing his witness through the written word. Year by year, week by week, we are blessed by that shared Word. And year by year, week by week, we have opportunities to be sharers of that Word where we live and work and learn. Today is the day of St. John—but it is also our day to be evangelists and friends of Jesus.

Now that third title, friend, is not officially in the name for this day on the church calendar. But it well might be—for in the pages of Scripture we discover in John a true friend of Jesus. Jesus is the friend of sinners. John knew how much Jesus loved him, and he tried to reflect that love by being a friend.

John often is there at the special times when not all of the Twelve are involved, such as on the Mount of Transfiguration. John is there to share the big moments, and he is there to do the little tasks. It is John, along with Peter, who is sent to get the donkey for Jesus to ride when He entered Jerusalem on Palm Sunday. It is John who helps to make the preparations for the Passover meal with Jesus in the Upper Room. John alone among the disciples goes with Jesus into the high priests' courtyard on the night of His arrest and trial. And it is John to whom Jesus gives responsibility for the care of His mother, Mary, in His word from the cross: "Behold, your mother!" As John himself writes, "From that hour the disciple took her to his own home" (Jn 19:27).

John is a friend of Jesus, willing to do his Lord's bidding. John is the kind of friend that stays close to his Master and who finds blessing in loving service to the one who loved him first and most. John's example is one for us to follow. A title of great honor is to be known as Jesus' friends (Jn 15:13–15), friends not only of Jesus but also friends for Jesus, which brings us to our text for today.

In the very last part of John's Gospel, he tells about some appearances of Jesus after His resurrection. One early morning the disciples are out fishing when someone calls to them from the shore. The first one to recognize Jesus is John. As he tells it, "That disciple whom Jesus loved therefore said to Peter, 'It is the Lord!'" (Jn 21:7). He heard the voice he knew, and responded to it. The account goes on to tell how Jesus shared breakfast on the shore with the disciples and blessed them with His presence. John knew Jesus was his Lord and his friend. In sharing that Lord and friend, John became the person we know and celebrate as apostle and evangelist.

"It is the Lord." The words are ours as well when we recognize Jesus coming to us in Word and Sacrament. May this third day of Christmas inspire us to follow the example of John—apostle, evangelist, friend—leading us in our own ways to be His workers, sharers of His message, friends of and for Jesus.

Rev. Gregory Wismar

The Holy Innocents

Holy Innocence!

Matthew 2:16–18

One of the loveliest and most winsome of the carols of the Christmas season is the Coventry Carol, a lullaby from the late Middle Ages. When we hear the haunting refrain "By, by, lully, lullay," we may think that the song is being addressed to the infant Christ Child as the Virgin Mary rocks Him gently to sleep. But that is not the situation at all. Actually, the song is a lament for one of the holy innocents, the young children of Bethlehem, who are about to be murdered because of the paranoid wrath of King Herod. The verses of the song, which was part of an old English sacred pageant sequence, tell the story. One verse says simply and poignantly:

> Herod the king, in his raging,
> Charged he hath this day
> His men of might, in his own sight,
> All young children to slay.

The sadness of the song comes through as the singer realizes that she cannot save the little child she knows is marked for death, but can only sing to it with a gentle lullaby.

St. Matthew, in a very few verses of his Gospel, also tells the story of the sorrowful tragedy of the holy innocents, who are remembered by the Church each year on December 28, as part of the three days after Christmas. Matthew writes that when the Magi do not return to Jerusalem with details regarding the new king of the Jews they had come to visit in Bethlehem, Herod senses that he has been duped by the visitors from the East. Whatever they had discovered in Bethlehem was something that they did not want to share with him. Whomever they had found there was not for him to know about. Herod did not take this slight by the Wise Men lightly. "They must have found the Messiah," he mused to himself. "I'd better do something about that."

Herod was a man of decision and action. He was responsible for some of the greatest building projects the world had seen, including the temple in Jerusalem and a network of mighty palaces and fortresses throughout his territories, including Masada and the Herodium, located near Bethlehem. He was also responsible for some of the most savage killings imaginable, including that of one of his wives, a number of his sons, and many of his friends and associates. Murder came easily to Herod. Although it may seem incomprehensible that a ruler would decree the death of all male babies in one of his towns, that action is totally in character for Herod the Great. He wanted no competition for his throne as the king of the Jews. So he decreed death for those holy, innocent little ones, who are sometimes referred to as the first martyrs for Christ.

The word *martyr* has a variety of meanings. In a wider sense it describes a witness, a person who has seen or done something and tells about it. Through the centuries, the word came to have a more specific meaning: a person who sacrificed his or her life in witnessing to Christ and to the Christian faith. The list of martyrs, when that definition is used, is remarkable. The Te Deum, one of the great canticles of the Church, speaks about "the noble army of martyrs" who praise God (*LSB*, p. 223). Although we may think mostly of adults as martyrs—from St. Stephen through most of the disciples of Jesus to the persecuted saints of the Early Church, on to the victims of the executions of the Reformation era and further to our own century—there have been countless children among the number of martyrs.

It is fitting, then, that the Church, since at least the fifth century after Christ, has taken a day each year to remember not only the slaughtered babes of Bethlehem but other young martyrs as well. These "sweet flowerets of the martyr band," as one hymn calls them, have lessons to share with us and encouragement to give us as well—lessons on persecution and pain, on praise, and on the promise of God.

The account of the holy innocents of Bethlehem reminds us that, from the very beginning of Jesus' earthly life, association with Him has had its consequences. The little ones of Bethlehem did not fully know the child of Mary, the Son of God; yet on His account their earthly lives were cut short. Herod probably justified his horrible action in some political way. Martin Luther conjectured, "The slaughter by Herod of all the children of Bethlehem and the region about was a piece of sheer barbarism, but doubt not that Herod would find a plausible defense so that people would regard it, not as tyranny, but as necessary severity. The world is a master of this art, when it goes against the Christians." In Luther's age and time, there were types of persecution of Christians for their faith. The types and forms may change from time to time, but no era is immune to them—not even our own.

As we come to the end of another calendar year, it would be good for us to reflect on the type of witness to our Lord that each of us has been in the past months. How have we dealt with persecution, if it has happened to us in any way, no matter how subtle? Have we stood up for our faith and been counted for the Lord? What kinds of witnesses (or martyrs, in the wide sense) have we been? In choosing appropriate calendar observances for the three days immediately following the celebration of the birth of Christ, the Church has chosen to highlight the sacrifice of Stephen, who was stoned to death; of John, who was exiled in his old age; and of the innocent little ones, who were killed by Herod's orders. In his writing about the holy innocents, Luther quotes these words of Jesus to His disciples: "The hour is coming when whoever kills you will think he is offering service to God" (Jn 16:2). That time has come before and may well come again before the Lord returns with His holy angels.

We connect great joy with the arrival of Jesus, the babe of Bethlehem, but there is pain as well. The Savior has come to take away the sins of the world, including our sins of anger and thoughtlessness regarding other people; but it will be at a price of pain. The advent of and prelude to that pain and suffering in fulfilling the Law for all people is remembered on the eighth day of Christmas, when the circumcision of Jesus takes place. His suffering will intensify throughout His life until the day of Good Friday, when it is completed on the cross of Calvary, as He dies to pay the price of our sins and the sins of all people. The job not accomplished by Herod will be completed by the Roman governor who eventually assumes the rule forfeited by one of Herod's sons. The shadow of the cross tempers the joy of Christmas with the sense of pain yet to come.

That pain is experienced not only by Jesus but by those who are close to Him as well. When His mother, Mary, comes to the temple at the time of her Son's presentation, the righteous man Simeon tells her that a sword will pierce her own soul too (Lk 2:35). Certainly, the death of the holy innocents caused great anguish to their parents and families. St. Matthew, as he writes his narrative, states that the whole nation was drawn into the pain of the slaughter. The grief after Herod's massacre is as great as it was at the time when the northern part of God's people were taken and dispersed by the Assyrians—that time when the weeping of Rachel, the mother of Israel, for her disappearing children was beyond consolation. Jeremiah had once described that anguish—and here it happened again in the sorrows of Bethlehem.

Yet beyond the pain there is something more: there is praise and promise. Although there is a theme of sadness to the day of the Holy Innocents, there is also a theme of triumph. Through the sacrifice of these children, a witness was made. Their martyrdom is recalled on this day each year; their heavenly reward is also remembered. As St. Augustine once preached: "For as today's feast reveals, in the measure with which malice in all its fury was poured out upon the holy children, did heaven's blessing stream down upon them." Appropriately, the Church has chosen Psalm 8 as the psalm of the day, in which the second verse reads: "Out of the mouth of babes and infants, You have established strength because of Your foes, to still the enemy and the avenger." Not long after the death of the infants at Bethlehem, Herod's death brought about a time when Mary and Joseph and the baby Jesus were able to return from Egypt to the land of God's promise. Their life went on. The child Jesus grew in strength and wisdom amid the sunny hills of Nazareth, far removed from the streets of Bethlehem and the terror and the sadness they had known. But the death of the little children was never forgotten. Today we join in praising God, as we remember them these many centuries after their tragic deaths.

The martyrdom of the holy innocents touches our hearts. It reminds us that senseless evil and sin are very much part of the world. It makes us aware all the more of the need of the Savior, the promised babe of Bethlehem, who lived and died and lives again for us, the one who brings us forgiveness of sins and the one whom it is our joy to serve (as Luther says) "in everlasting righteousness, innocence, and blessedness" (*Luther's Small Catechism*, p. 16). God has promised the presence of His Holy Spirit in our hearts and lives as we discover ways to be witnesses to Christ our Lord. By God's grace, holy innocence is our calling, however long our earthly life may be. May we find encouragement and blessing in recalling the Holy Innocents, looking forward to the heavenly meeting with them and the shared privilege of praising Jesus, the baby born in Bethlehem for time and for eternity.

Rev. Gregory Just Wismar

Why Are You Weeping, Rachel?

Matthew 2:13–18

Christmas in the United States wears two faces. Christmas letters describe perfect families with no mention of the sin. We sing "Joy to the World!" and "Good Christian Men, Rejoice," yet read of murder, violence, and rape in the daily newspaper. Most people living in the United States celebrate Christmas, yet 53 percent of the United States population is involved in a non-Christian religion.[11] We proclaim peace on earth while an ambassador tries to implement peace talks somewhere in the world. It is the fourth day of Christmas, yet many of our Christmas trees are already thrown out or packed away. Merchants pass judgment on how "good" this Christmas was, using sales dollars as the standard.

Perhaps we who really do know the "reason for the season" are partly guilty for the fake Christmas around us. We present our neighbors and friends with a veneer of joy, without first proclaiming why baby Jesus was born. We repeat the good news sung by angels, but how many sermons have you heard on weeping Rachel? Rachel is an important person in Matthew's version of the Christmas story. Listen to this—it is the rest of the Christmas story. *(Read Mt 2:13–18.)*

Who is this Rachel? Why is she weeping? And why do we usually ignore her?

Rachel's Story

Perhaps you remember Rachel from Sunday School (Genesis 29–35). She met Jacob when he rolled the stone away from the well so that she could water her father's sheep. Jacob wanted to marry Rachel, but Laban, her father, tricked him. Jacob worked seven years to earn Rachel, but on the morning after the wedding found out that he had married her sister, Leah. So Jacob had to work for seven more years to "earn" Rachel. Rachel must have wept over that.

Rachel probably wept over the circumstances in which her husband's name changed from Jacob to Israel. Rachel must have wept when she could not have children, even while Leah and two other "second wives" gave Jacob ten sons and a daughter. Finally, Rachel's womb opened, and she gave birth to Joseph. Then she died weeping, giving birth to Benjamin. Jacob buried her near Bethlehem. Over

---

11 *Good News* no. 8 (St. Louis: Concordia Mission Society): 10.

the years, there was a lot of sadness in Jacob's family, and there was a lot of weeping, but that is not what Jeremiah was talking about.

More than a thousand years after Rachel died, after the children of Israel—including Rachel's descendants—were enslaved in Egypt, after the Exodus under Moses, after the time of King David, after the civil war that tore the nation apart, the time came when the people of Judah were carried off into captivity in Babylon. As they were led away in chains, they were led past the site of Rachel's grave. Jeremiah says that Rachel cried from her grave: "A voice is heard in Ramah, lamentation and bitter weeping. Rachel is weeping for her children; she refuses to be comforted for her children, because they are no more" (Jer 31:15).

In our text, Matthew, inspired by the Holy Spirit, does something remarkable. He takes a historical event from six hundred years before Jesus' birth and applies it to the children of Rachel who died soon after Jesus was born. Not only did Rachel cry from her grave as her children were marched off into Babylonian captivity, but she also wept again as her children were slaughtered by Herod's swords. The Holy Innocents died. Rachel wept. That is the rest of the Christmas story. Jesus came into a world of sin. The devil aggressively tried to kill the baby Jesus—before He could grow up and fight Satan at the cross. Our world is still full of sin. The devil still seeks those he can devour (1 Pet 5:8). Innocent babies still die. *(Insert current abortion statistics from your area.)* Listen! Do you hear Rachel weeping? I do.

THE CHRISTMAS STORY

Matthew's Gospel is the story of how God came to conquer sin—your sin and mine. Jesus came to live in a world that threatened His life just as it threatens yours. Matthew tells us of Herod's bloody swords so that he can also tell us how God the Father sent an angel to protect Jesus, Mary, and Joseph (Mt 2:13, 19–20) so that Jesus could carry out His mission of dying for the sins of the world. Matthew and Luke both tell the story of the birth of Jesus as part of the larger story of Jesus' living, preaching, teaching, healing, dying, rising, and ascending.

Our world does not want to hear it. Our world does not want to hear about sin. Sometimes we don't want to hear it either, do we? But there is no Christmas without Good Friday. We condemn people around us to die forever when we permit them to have a pretend Christmas. A Christmas without Rachel weeping may as well be built on Santa and Rudolph.

Ours is a world that needs Jesus in the manger and on the cross and at the empty tomb. Our world needs Jesus risen from the dead. Our world needs Jesus because Rachel still weeps. Rachel weeps and so do you, don't you? Child abuse is real. Spousal abuse is real. Cancer is real. Abuse of drugs and alcohol is real. Fornication and adultery are real. Lack of thankfulness to our good Lord is real.

Slander and theft and greed are real. Poor stewardship and lack of mission are real. Death is real.

Jesus was born to deal with our real world. Jesus was born to dry Rachel's tears. Jesus lived and died and rose again to dry your tears. At our house this year, we hung only one ornament on our Christmas tree. The only ornament on our tree is this spike. Christmas is real at our house because Good Friday and Easter are real.

Much of Christmas is already in the trash can. Christmas can be a sham used to make people feel good without reminding them of their basic problem—sin. This morning you and I are at Rachel's tomb. We hear her weeping. We remember our weeping. We know that our false Christmases—our false lives—bring tears to God's eyes. We know, too, that the real Christmas is God—the Father, Son, and Holy Spirit—dealing with our sin.

Let's celebrate a real Christmas, saying with the hymn writer:

> As Your coming was in peace,
> Quiet, full of gentleness,
> Let the same mind dwell in me
> Which is Yours eternally.
>
> Bruise for me the Serpent's head
> That, set free from doubt and dread,
> I may cling to You in faith,
> Safely kept through life and death.
>
> Then when You will come again
> As the glorious king to reign,
> I with joy will see Your face,
> Freely ransomed by Your grace."
> (*LSB* 352:4–6)

Rev. Warren E. Messmann

Occasions

Anniversary of a Church

God, Our Help and Our Hope

Psalm 90:1–4; 46:1–3

In 1896, the year Trinity congregation began, Henry Ford's first car appeared on the streets of Detroit, Michigan, and Grover Cleveland was president of the United States. Canada was a young, growing country only twenty-nine years old. Its population was about five million, compared to thirty million today. Meanwhile, Trinity's founding fathers built a small church a few miles southeast of here.

Our loving triune God has blessed this congregation for a century, and today many members and friends converge here to praise and thank Him. May the Holy Spirit open our ears and hearts to hear His Word as we direct our thoughts to "O God, our help in ages past, Our hope for years to come" (*LSB* 733:1).

O GOD, OUR HELP IN AGES PAST

"Before the mountains were brought forth, or ever You had formed the earth and the world, from everlasting to everlasting You are God" (Ps 90:2). Included in God's creation is the Qu'Appelle Valley with all its beauty, lakes, grass, shrubs, and hills—its domestic animals as well as its wildlife. In British Columbia we have the Okanagan Valley, Okanagan Lake, Skaha Lake, and orchards, flanked by tree-covered mountains. Arizona boasts of the Grand Canyon. We have majestic mountains of various sizes and shapes, but all with a durability that suggests permanence. They have existed for generations—for centuries. They continue with no apparent change.

The psalmist says, "Before the mountains were brought forth"—before the world, our globe, came into being—what was there? Who was there? Our eternal God was there, "from everlasting to everlasting." He had no beginning and no end. "For a thousand years in Your sight are but as yesterday when it is past, or as a watch in the night" (Ps 90:4). (A watch is four hours.) Time does not exist for God. He is above time; beyond time. "Lord, You have been our dwelling place in all generations" (Ps 90:1).

God is our refuge, our shelter, and our protection. Noah and his immediate family, under divine direction, found refuge in the ark as the waters rose during the flood. The Lord was the refuge and protector of the Israelites as He provided a passage for them through the Red Sea, but He caused its waters to collapse on the Egyptians. He was the Protector and Savior of Shadrach, Meshach, and Abednego in the fiery furnace. That is the God in whom the early Christian settlers believed, whom they worshiped, whose Word they wanted to hear, and to whose honor and glory they built Trinity Lutheran Church a century ago.

A century seems like a long time to us mortals. It is, however, less than a speck, only an instant compared to the immense, incomprehensible eternity of God. Yet God guided and protected Trinity Lutheran Church during this century. To be sure, there were problems, difficulties, and troubles. The psalm says, "You return man to dust and say, 'Return, O children of man!' " (Ps 90:3). Scores of members have departed this life. Many others have moved, perhaps because of illness or a job. During this century there have been two world wars and innumerable brush-fire wars. The Depression lingered. There were droughts and epidemics. In other parts of the world there were earthquakes, floods, and fires. Here, dust storms and snow blizzards battered the church. Yet by the grace of God, Trinity stood and still stands. So now we celebrate its centennial.

As God fed Israel in the wilderness for forty years, so He gave spiritual nourishment to this congregation for two-and-a-half times that long. Fourteen pastors and a number of vacancy pastors have served during the first century of the congregation's existence. Young and old have heard the creation account.

Man's origin was not a slow, gradual development—he is not a product of evolution. "God created man in His own image, in the image of God He created him; male and female He created them" (Gen 1:27).

The Bible speaks of sin and of death. "For all have sinned and fall short of the glory of God" (Rom 3:23). "Therefore, just as sin came into the world through one man, and death through sin, and so death spread to all men because all sinned" (Rom 5:12). "For the wages of sin is death" (Rom 6:23).

God's Son led a perfect life, and paid a painful price for our transgressions. He bled to cleanse us from all sins and died that we might live. "The Son of Man came not to be served but to serve, and to give His life as a ransom for many" (Mk 10:45). "For the Son of Man came to seek and to save the lost" (Lk 19:10). Jesus said, "I am the way, and the truth, and the life. No one comes to the Father except through Me" (Jn 14:6).

What comfort there is in these words! God has given you a century of blessings. Have you received them, availed yourselves of them? Appreciated them? Shared them with others? All need God's Word as a warning, for comfort, and for growth.

Our Hope for Years to Come

In the last one hundred years, there have been frightening times. We have seen many rapid changes: Unemployment Insurance, Family Allowance, Medicare, and Canada Pension came into being. Many new inventions are now obsolete. We have excellent communication. We can easily and quickly phone someone on another continent. An event may occur on the other side of the world and instantly we see it on our television. A few generations ago, people had boxlike cameras with which they took black-and white-snapshots. Today, with camcorders and VCRs, we can hear our own voices and see ourselves in color and in motion on the television screen. A six-hour flight will take us to Europe. Computers can bring us information from anywhere in the world instantly. Put the right card into the right slot and presto! We have cash. There are attractive offers—"buy now, pay later" and "no down payment, no interest"—but there are also warning signals. "Buyer, beware" and "if it's too good to be true, it probably isn't true."

People commit old sins in new ways with new tricks. In 1996, TWA flight 800 exploded, killing 230 people, and a bomb blast rocked the Olympics in Atlanta. Bomb scares echo in many parts of the world. Immorality, abuses, and murders continue. The concerned citizen asks what is next? The confident Christian says with the psalmist, "My help comes from the LORD, who made heaven and earth" (Ps 121:2).

Psalm 46 speaks of cataclysmic upheavals. "The earth gives way," "the mountains be moved into the heart of the sea," "waters roar and foam," and "mountains tremble" (vv. 2–3)—what splashing, bubbling, agitation, roaring of waves! God is above all of these; He is in control! With nations possessing powerful bombs and the end of all things approaching, we can expect such conditions and worse. No caves, no man-made shelters, no drugs will prevent the Lord's second coming on Judgment Day! To whom shall we go? We go to our everlasting, loving God, our Creator, Redeemer, and Sanctifier.

Not only is Trinity Lutheran Church beginning its second century, but we are also nearing the threshold of the third millennium in the Christian era. Our triune God, Father, Son, and Holy Spirit, will be our dwelling place—"our refuge and strength, a very present help in trouble" (Ps 46:1) in the next millennium. The divine Son of God has not only carried all our sins, paid for them, and died for them, but also rose victoriously! He has overcome the enemy. "We know that Christ being raised from the dead will never die again; death no longer has dominion over Him" (Rom 6:9). With the apostle Paul we jubilate: "But thanks be to God, who gives us the victory through our Lord Jesus Christ" (1 Cor 15:57). What an incentive, what motivating words not only to rely on the divine Helper but also to work for Him in the years ahead. At the close of 1 Corinthians 15, in which the apostle speaks of Christ's resurrection from the dead and also our resurrection, he adds words that encourage us to hear and obey: "Therefore, my beloved brothers, be steadfast, immovable, always abounding in the work of the Lord, knowing that in the Lord your labor is not in vain" (1 Cor 15:58).

> O God, our help in ages past,
> Our hope for years to come,
> Our shelter from the stormy blast,
> And our eternal home. (*LSB* 733:1)

Rev. Leander Arndt

Ordination or Installation

Runaway Preacher

Jonah 1–4

The day we receive our call to follow Christ, we face the temptation to run away and reject our call. That is true on the day of our Baptism into Christ; the day of a pastor's ordination into the Office of the Holy Ministry; and the day of a pastor's installation.

Of course, we're not the first ones to be tempted to run away. We pastors are in the prophetic and apostolic ministry. Moses ran away and stayed away for forty years. Elijah ran away from the wicked queen Jezebel. Jesus' disciples took one look at the soldiers who came to arrest Him and ran away. John Mark ran away from St. Paul during a missionary journey (Acts 13:13; 15:38).

The Lord called Jonah to travel east to Nineveh on a preaching mission. But stubborn Jonah went in the opposite direction. He ran away to the coast of the Mediterranean Sea. He went down to the dock, bought a ticket, paid his fare, and boarded a ship headed for Spain.

"All aboard!" Soon the winds started gusting. A terrible storm raged. But Jonah was below deck, sleeping. (Centuries later, Jesus, too, would sleep in a boat during a storm while those around Him were alarmed.)

The sailors, though pagans, discerned that the powers of heaven were angry at someone on board. A guilty person had precipitated the foul weather. To find out who it was, they cast lots. Perhaps all the passengers and crew took a pebble from a jar. Who got the marked pebble? Jonah, of course. God would not let him hide among the unbelievers.

The sailors quizzed Jonah. "Where are you from?" "What have you done?" Jonah told them that he worshiped the true God, the Creator of all things. He had formed the heavens and the earth and all that is in them in six short days. He was in control; the storm was the result of His anger, and there was no place where one could hide from His eyes. The storm worsened, and the sailors trembled with terror as they learned of this supreme God. They pleaded, "What shall we do?"

Jonah said, "Throw me overboard." This sounds like an act of self-sacrifice. Jonah was willing to give up his own life to spare the pagan sailors from certain death. (Similarly, Jesus would give up His own life to save those who were far from God.)

But for Jonah, being cast overboard might also have been a way to elude his call from God. Four times in the four chapters of this book, Jonah asks to die. Death is one way desperate people may try to escape from God. But God is Lord over life and death, and His plans for Jonah were plans of life. So God ordered a large fish (or whale; the Hebrew word could mean either) to swallow Jonah and preserve him alive for three days and three nights. Then God ordered the creature to spew Jonah onto the dry land so he could resume his call to the prophetic office. This three-day rescue from death to life is the famous "sign of Jonah" that Jesus referred to His own resurrection. Both really happened: just as Jonah's story is a historical account, so also the resurrection of Jesus Christ is a fact of world history. And Jesus' self-sacrifice and resurrection on the third day are what make possible the ministries of modern prophets as well as ancient ones such as Jonah.

In the Sacrament of Baptism each Christian descends into a watery grave, as did Jonah in the depths of the sea, and dies with Christ. But the Lord over death and life has plans for each of us, and those plans include life—resurrection life. In Baptism each of us is miraculously raised up out of death to new life with Christ. As with Jonah, the life we now have is a direct result of this resurrection. And the purpose of this new lease on life we have been given is to respond to God's call—not to run away, but to carry out our call by running to Nineveh, or wherever else God has called us to serve.

The Ninevites, too, received a kind of resurrection. Warned that God would strike their city down, they repented, and their death sentence was commuted. God's plans for them, too, were plans for life. That is a picture of a pastor's ministry: to call people to repentance so that they may escape God's judgment and instead receive God's new resurrection life.

The account of Jonah shows that God's call includes a call to suffer. It's part of the job. Take, for example, a week in the life of a pastor (at its worst):

It's Monday morning. You wake up to a gray day. Monday is always gray, even when the sun shines, because it's the anticlimax to Sunday, the day of resurrection. You feel like Jonah after his vine withered, thinking that perhaps your ministry has been ineffective, wasted. It's slow-down day. Throw a few stones at yourself. It's hard to preoccupy yourself with busyness to cover up this self-inspection and self-condemnation.

As the week progresses, you begin to get caught up in your pastoral activities. And the first person you meet showers you with compliments. He praises you to the highest heaven. It feels wonderful! You love it. It is just what you need. But before long you feel guilty. Am I inclined to conform to the compliments and comments of people? Am I my own man or God's man?

Many people find it hard to take a neutral view of their pastor. They either love him or hate him. Often the same people do both at the same time.

And then there are some whose love turns cold. If they leave the church, you feel deserted and abandoned. And you blame yourself. What did I do wrong? Did I give offense? Did they take offense? In either case, a chasm forms. So you're tempted to despair and run away.

You visit hospitals, nursing homes, and funeral homes. You listen to parents grieve when their teenagers get into trouble. You may be called to counsel a pregnant girl and her boyfriend as they pour out their hearts to you.

When people face crises in their lives, they put God on trial. They accuse Him of injustice, capriciousness, or outright evil. It's your job as pastor to proclaim the biblical view of God as good and gracious, though that grace is hidden in strange forms: the Gospel Word of a weak and crucified Christ; the resurrection power that comes through water poured out in the triune name; the power of forgiveness and resurrection in pieces of bread and sips of wine that are Christ's body and blood. But the Gospel never feels adequate because crises and tragedy are so loud and the God of the Gospel seems so silent and meek.

One day you look at yourself in the mirror and ask, "Have I worked hard enough in the ministry?" And suddenly you sense, "While I'm preaching to others that we are saved by grace, I'm living as though I'm saved by works."

You work hard preparing for Sunday's sermon. And you're expected to describe the indescribable, put the infinite into finite words. But the words elude you, and the voice to say those words is too small and weak to match the enormity of the Gospel. When you do find the words, you recall that you spoke those same words just last week. You're repeating yourself again and again.

In view of the life of the pastor at its worst, it's no surprise to you that not many people want to become pastors. Yet—it's paradoxical. Doesn't everyone want to be a pastor at the best of times? Pastor *(name)*, you are a part of this congregation. You share the highest moments of life with this community of saints.

You walk the floor with a nervous father in the maternity ward while the mother brings a new life into the world. Later, you gently take that young life into your arms, make the sign of the cross, pour water on the forehead, and say, "I baptize you in the name of the Father and of the Son and of the Holy Spirit." You are there when eternal life for this child begins.

You are there when that child is confirmed and receives, for the first time, the body and blood of Jesus Christ, a foretaste of the feast to come. You are there when that young adult and his or her beloved come to the altar and you pronounce them husband and wife until death parts them. You are there for their anniversaries as well. And you are there when the members of this congregation enter glory and the angels flutter their wings and say, "Look who's coming up to join the choir." And the angels sing.

Pastor *(name)*, you are there for every one of these high moments in your people's lives. You are there when people look for love and forgiveness. The boss's door may be closed when an employee makes a mistake. The spouse's door may be closed when anger takes over. The parent's door may close when children misbehave or misspeak. The children's door may close when parents lose patience and get angry. Doors close and slam in people's faces. There is a lack of love and forgiveness in the world. The love of many has grown cold.

But you, pastor, are called to close other doors—for example, to retain the sins of the impenitent, to block the door of divorce sought by a couple who needs to go the way of repentance, to rebuke the couple living together before marriage. But even when you shut doors to sin and harm, it is so that people will turn to the open door of God—the door that leads to reconciliation. You are there to keep that door open at all times. You open the door of forgiveness. You offer words of assurance and love. You bestow forgiveness every time you pronounce the words of absolution in the Divine Service and every time you distribute the Lord's Supper. Sunday after Sunday it's your God-ordained call to swing open the door of the Gospel, the ever-open door to God.

Your call as a pastor is to proclaim that God loved us so much that He sent His own Son, Jesus, to die to pay for our sins. And now in His love He forgives His penitent children freely and completely. Today your congregation and fellow pastors are affirming this call. Your congregation is promising to respect your office, support your ministry, and follow your leadership under God. You are entrusted with the keys to God's kingdom. In this place you are the under-shepherd who guides the flock on behalf of the Good Shepherd, to whom we all must one day give an account. Your holy office is a somber responsibility but also the highest honor. Never run away from it!

No one will dispute the difficulties you face as you carry out your office as pastor. Nor is it always easy for God's people to serve under the leadership of the pastors they call as overseers. Remember that when God called Jonah, He did not induce him to accept by promising an easy, painless task. Take for granted that struggle and hard work go hand-in-hand with your call.

But our Lord Jesus promises to stay with you. He will bless your efforts, both now and in the future. The means of grace may appear weak and futile in the face of the formidable powers at work in this world, but they are the power of God to salvation. Although you're tempted to despair, give up, and run away, God will continue to work through His Word and Sacraments, on you as well as on your people. God's forgiveness re-creates you. His forgiveness strengthens you and renews you.

You and this congregation are here for one another. You're here, Pastor *(name)*, for the members of this congregation. You're here for the community of saints in this place. And, church members, you're here for Pastor *(name)*. You're all here for one another. But most important, Jesus says, "I will always be here for you. I will never leave you nor forsake you. You may want to run from Me, but as I sought out Jonah, I will seek you out, bring you through death to new life, and use you to proclaim My name to the salvation of many souls. I will never run from you!"

Rev. Karl Schuessler

Christian Education

The Greatest Gift You Can Give

Deuteronomy 6:1–9

At one time or another, every parent here today has probably wondered: "What is the greatest gift I can give my child?" Think about it! What might that gift be? Is it a well-rounded education? If so, special effort would be made to live in a community with good schools, to provide piano and dance lessons, to encourage sports activities, and so on. Is it a happy and pleasant childhood? If so, special effort would be made to spend quality time with your children, to provide a home life with minimal stress and conflict, and to plan exciting family activities and vacations.

What is the greatest gift you can give your child? I suggest it is more than a well-rounded education and a happy and pleasant childhood—important as these are, I suggest the greatest gift you can give your child is the gift of Jesus. Let God's Word of forgiveness in Jesus Christ be, as our text says, upon your heart as a parent so you may impress that Gospel upon your children.

EDUCATION IS NOT INOCULATION

The problem, however, is that often parents fail to recognize the ongoing nature of this task. Do you ever think of religious education as a kind of "inoculation"—a one-time or short-term event that "exposes" your children to Christianity in the same way he or she may be exposed to chicken pox—to get it out of the way at an early age? Once he's been exposed, we figure, then he's had his lifelong dosage and we've done our job as parents.

The newspapers ran a story of a school bus driver who got lost driving a group of gifted children on an unfamiliar route. In frustration, she returned to the school, dropped the children off at the front steps, and told them, "You're gifted— you figure out how to get home." Fortunately, a woman living across the street invited the stranded children inside to call their parents. "The kids were just floating around out there in the cold afternoon," she said. "I couldn't just leave them alone out there like that." Because of their experience, these children didn't want to ride the bus again.

The same thing happens to children whose parents attempt "religious inoculation"—they are left stranded in the cold. These children are offered a short-term solution that delivers only short-term results. Once they grow up, they don't want to ride the religious bus anymore. What's the greatest gift you could ever give your child? It's not a religious inoculation but a Christian education! And a Christian education is found only through the teaching of God's love for us in Jesus Christ.

This is the education God wanted for His people when they came to the Promised Land. Our text is what God told Moses to tell the people. Note the ways in which they are to keep the commandments on their hearts: "You shall teach them diligently to your children, and shall talk of them when you sit in your house, and when you walk by the way, and when you lie down, and when you rise." And two things Jewish people still do: "You shall bind them as a sign on your hand, and they shall be as frontlets between your eyes. You shall write them on the doorposts of your house and on your gates" (vv. 7–9). Devout Jews wear small leather packets with Scripture in them on their forehead and arm when they pray and put small boxes with Scripture on their doorjamb so they can touch it when they come and go. Teaching children to "love the LORD your God with all your heart and with all your soul and with all your might" (v. 5) is not an inoculation but an ongoing education.

SPIRITUAL FORMATION

Ken Precht, a Lutheran schoolteacher and principal, testifies to how the Lord used his first-grade teacher in the Lutheran day school he attended. He remembers well the important role she played in his spiritual formation as a youngster. Nearly forty years later, Precht attended a teachers' convention where the speaker asked each person to think of a Lutheran schoolteacher or Sunday School teacher who had taught them the faith as a child. Participants then were asked to sing "Jesus Loves Me," substituting that teacher's name for "the Bible" in the phrase "the Bible tells me so." Who do you suppose was at that convention seated next to Precht? Yes, his first-grade teacher, now retired but still actively teaching the faith!

The love that every parent and every teacher of the faith throughout countless generations have told their children about is the Savior's love that has no bounds. It is the love of a God who cares so much for you and me that He sent His only-begotten Son to a cross, that whoever believes in Him will not perish but have eternal life. In Christ Jesus, your sins are no more, and His forgiveness is yours forever. That is God's love for you and that is the joyful Good News He has given you to teach to your children.

From one generation to the next, God's salvation in Christ Jesus is passed from parent to child and from teacher to student. Again and again the story of God's love for us in Christ Jesus is spoken. In this repetition, we see the continuous and ongoing nature of our Lord's love for us. He doesn't just inoculate us. Rather, He sticks with His people until the end of time. And so, also, we begin to see the nature of our task as Christian parents and teachers—not to inoculate our children with Christianity but to provide for their continuous and ongoing nurture in the Christian faith.

Lives Are Changed

Recently, Dr. James Dobson, noted Christian psychologist, was asked why we put children through the agony of learning when the human mind forgets some 80 percent of whatever it has learned within a few months. He listed four reasons: first, because it provides the basic self-discipline and self-control needed to function in adult life; second, that even if a person can't recall the exact material needed at least he knows where to look for it; third, we don't forget 100 percent of what we learn since the most important facts do find a place in our permanent memory; finally, perhaps the most significant reason that learning is important is because we are changed by what we learn. He writes: "Learning produces alterations in values, attitudes, and concepts that do not fade in time."

Ongoing Christian learning produces changes in values, attitudes, and concepts that will not fade in time either. That's why our text says we are to "teach diligently" the Lord's words to our children. "Teach diligently" has an urgent and ongoing sense to it. In fact, in the original Hebrew, it is related to the word for repetition. We teach the Lord's Word diligently to our children by repetition—by telling of God's love for them in Christ Jesus again and again and again from Baptism to adulthood.

"Teaching diligently" begins in the home as we teach our children how to pray at bedtime and before meals, as we read them Bible stories from a children's Bible or storybook again and again, and as we conduct family worship. Then, the church is enlisted in the process—through Sunday School, midweek school, confirmation instruction—and, most effectively, through a Lutheran day school such as the Lord has given us here. Through these means, Christian parents can teach their children of Jesus Christ and His precious love and forgiveness so these beloved children will remain firm in the Christian faith for the rest of their lives.

And what a glorious thing it is to witness the faith life of a child whose parents have raised him or her in God's Word and have themselves believed and taught it. St. Paul charges the young preacher Timothy to stick with what he learned long ago as a little child. "But as for you," Paul says, "continue in what you have learned and have firmly believed, knowing from whom you learned it and how from childhood you have been acquainted with the sacred writings" (2 Tim 3:14–15).

Now and Forever

Perhaps your child is well beyond the infant stage. Perhaps you feel it is too late to start training him or her in the faith. It is never too late, my friends. As long as the Lord has given you that child's body and mind to love and care for, He has also given you that child's soul to nurture and strengthen in the faith. Today is the day to begin. "Behold, now is the favorable time," says St. Paul; "behold, now is the day of salvation" (2 Cor 6:2). The Word of God that you teach your children today, dear parents, is the one thing in their lives that will truly last forever. As Isaiah declares: "The grass withers, the flower fades, but the word of our God will stand forever" (Is 40:8).

Long after you and I are gone and our children have raised their children and have seen their children's children come also to the baptismal font of life, nothing else will matter but that we here today taught our young ones to know Jesus Christ as their Savior from sin. Nothing else will matter—certainly not the money we saved, the businesses we ran, the houses we lived in, or even the friends and memories we shared—none of that will matter. The only thing that will matter will be the Gospel—the saving Gospel of Jesus Christ, which has brought life to us and to our children. That is the greatest gift you can give your child—the gift of life, real life, in Jesus Christ.

Rev. Jon D. Vieker

All Is Vanity apart from Christ

Ecclesiastes 1:1–14; Luke 19:41–48

He had it all! He reigned over Israel when she was at the pinnacle of her wealth and worldly prestige. Neighboring countries paid him tribute. There was peace within his borders. His citizens lacked for nothing. "And Judah and Israel lived in safety, from Dan even to Beersheba, every man under his vine and under his fig tree, all the days of Solomon" (1 Ki 4:25). He had it all! His name was King Solomon.

Solomon had forty thousand stalls of horses for his chariots and twelve thousand horsemen. According to the Scriptures:

> Solomon's wisdom surpassed the wisdom of all the people of the east and all the wisdom of Egypt. For he was wiser than all other men. . . . He also spoke 3,000 proverbs, and his songs were 1,005. He spoke of trees, from the cedar that is in Lebanon to the hyssop that grows out of the wall. He spoke also of beasts, and of birds, and of reptiles, and of fish. And people of all nations came to hear the wisdom of Solomon, and from all the kings of the earth, who had heard of his wisdom. (1 Ki 4:30–34)

THE WISDOM OF SOLOMON

Solomon had it all. He was an educated man—a botanist, zoologist, astronomer, philosopher, and statesman. His wisdom and knowledge were coveted by everyone. I wish that I had the wisdom of Solomon at times. Make no mistake about it—his education, wealth, honor, prestige, and wisdom were all gifts from God. Yet with all that Solomon had been given, he penned some of the darkest words in all of Scripture: "Vanity of vanities, says the Preacher, vanity of vanities! All is vanity. What does man gain by all the toil at which he toils under the sun?" (Eccl 1:2–3).

Nothing! For all his toils under the sun, man has nothing. It is all meaningless, empty, vain, and full of frustration. What a strange way to begin a school year or talk about Christian education! "Vanity of vanities, all is vanity." All of your work is useless. Your pursuit of knowledge, of excellence, of achievement—it is all a chasing after the wind. That's what Solomon was inspired to write by the Holy Spirit: "I have seen everything that is done under the sun, and behold, all is vanity and a striving after wind. . . . I said in my heart, 'I have acquired great wisdom, surpassing all who were over Jerusalem before me, and my heart has had great experience of wisdom and knowledge.' And I applied my heart to know wisdom and to know madness and folly. I perceived that this also is but a striving after wind. For in much wisdom is much vexation, and he who increases knowledge increases sorrow" (Eccl 1:14, 16–18). "Vanity of vanities, all is vanity."

Why should we go to school at all? Listening to Solomon, arguably the wisest and smartest and most knowledgeable man who ever lived, we may be tempted to conclude, "What's the point of anything that we do?" What's the point of all the long hours you teachers will expend preparing lessons in history, science, geography, and mathematics if it is all vanity—meaningless? What's the point of teaching self-discipline and demanding excellence if it's all meaningless? For that matter, what's the point of education at all?

Nothing, apart from Christ

Simply put, there is no point to anything that we do apart from Christ. Every gift of God can be transformed into an idol. Our Lutheran day school, our approach to education, our philosophy of learning, our curriculum, our desire to build a school of academic excellence—all of these things become idols apart from Christ. Every good thing becomes a demon where faith in Christ is not above everything else. In another place, Solomon wrote, "The fear of the LORD is the beginning of wisdom" (Ps 111:10). The Lord of whom he spoke is the Lord Jesus. To fear the Lord is to know Him, to trust Him, to look to Him for everything, to believe in Him as the "one thing needful." This is the beginning of wisdom.

None of us would admit to having idols, but we are all threatened by them. You can judge what the idols are that threaten your life by considering all of those things that you would never relinquish. What are the non-negotiables of your life? What do you insist on having? "A god means that from which we are to expect all good and in which we are to take refuge in all distress," wrote Luther in the Large Catechism (part I, paragraph 2; *Concordia*, p. 359). If it is not an idol that threatens you, why are you so miserable when it is taken away? You see, the problem is not with the "good thing" that we value, but how much value we place upon it.

There was nothing more precious to the Jews of Jesus' day than their interpretation of God's Mosaic Law. They valued their service to the Law (as they understood it) above all things. That's what Jesus addressed in the Gospel for today. They were zealous. They added their own rules to God's Word and insisted upon strict observance. But Jesus called their belief in their interpretation of God's Law blasphemy and an abomination to the Lord.

Why? Because all their sincerely held, passionate beliefs concerning their law and their own obedience to it did not have Christ at its center. Their law became an idol, a demon, for them because Christ was missing. They did not see their sin. They did not see their pride. They did not see their self-righteousness. Therefore, they did not see their need for Him who alone could make for their peace by the blood of His cross. The same could be said of us whenever any "good thing" in our lives takes possession of us. We are blinded and do not know the things that make for our peace.

The Law's Fulfillment

Think about the idolatrous faith of the Jews of Jesus' time. What could be greater than God's own Law? What could be greater than wanting to serve God's Law? What could be greater than marshaling all our powers to try to obey the Law? However, no sinful person can truly obey the Law and win God's favor. Christ is greater than the Law! He is the Law's fulfillment! To be a Christian is to believe in Him alone. The Law was fulfilled in His death when He took the punishment for our sin. His death alone made peace between the sinner and God. Most of the Jews in Jesus' day didn't believe this. They believed they were serving God by their sincere attempts to keep their Law, but they were really serving the devil. This is why Jesus wept over Jerusalem when He drew near her, saying, "Would that you, even you, had known on this day the things that make for peace! But now they are hidden from your eyes" (Lk 19:42).

He stood before them—the One who alone could make for their peace—but they rejected Him. As a result, the temple in Jerusalem was destroyed and the city was nearly leveled to the ground forty years after Jesus spoke His warning. What about us? As the hymn writer put it, "Earth has no pleasure I would share. Yea, heav'n itself were void and bare If Thou, Lord, wert not near me" (*LSB* 708:1). All is vanity apart from Christ.

Jesus stands before us each day in this place, not only on Sunday morning, but each day in the life of our school and congregation through Bible story, catechism, and liturgy. He is the one thing needful. We know of no Jesus except that Jesus who comes to us through His Word to give life and salvation in the forgiveness of sins. Apart from Him all that we do is vanity, no matter how noble the pursuit. The Lutheran understanding of the Gospel is what, more than anything else, sets apart a Lutheran school from all others. We sinners are justified by faith in Christ alone. The catechism expounds the Gospel from Scripture and teaches us to know ourselves and to know our Savior aright. Through liturgy and hymnody we learn to approach Christ in every time of need. The mercy of God in Christ teaches us to love one another and to dwell together with one another in unconditional forgiveness, bearing one another's weaknesses. These teachings come from Christ and make for our peace.

The idolatry that resided in the hearts of the Jews of which Jesus spoke in today's Gospel is deeply imbedded within our hearts as well. It threatens us as much as it threatened them. But this is the Good News: Jesus wept over Jerusalem in love for all her lost sinners. He desired only one thing—to draw her to Himself, to call her to repentance, to forgive her sins, to cover her with the robe of His righteousness. He yearns to do the same for us. He doesn't force Himself upon us. He loves, gently and tenderly, like a faithful husband who gives His very life for his bride. Faith alone receives Him! By faith we have peace with God through our Lord Jesus Christ. Apart from Christ, all is vanity! But with Christ—His Word, His Baptism, His Absolution, His Supper—we have all we need. As we consider all that we do in this place, all that we desire for our school, our children, and our lives, fix your ears upon this promise: "He who did not spare His own Son but gave Him up for us all, how will He not also with Him graciously give us all things?" (Rom 8:32 NKJV).

Rev. Peter C. Bender

Day of Thanksgiving

To Be Content: Four Options

Philippians 4:10–13

A few years ago a woman from the Soviet Union visited New York City. She was not too impressed by what she saw. She said Moscow also had a large airport and a magnificent subway system. But when she was taken into a supermarket, she stopped, looked around, and simply broke down and cried.

I think of that woman and people in other countries of the world where there is a shortage of food. Then I think of how discontented I sometimes feel when I cannot find the exact brand of food I want in the supermarket. It makes me feel sheepish, to say the least. I feel even worse when, though living in the lap of plenty, I become envious of what others have.

Here it is Thanksgiving. We all want to be happy, and most of us are; but too often our joys are tinged with apprehension. Will our happiness end before the day is out? That phone ringing—I hope it isn't an accident; I hope they're just late. I wonder if someone here today won't be here next Thanksgiving. I would truly be happy if only . . . . Are we so dependent on circumstances that we cannot be content for longer than a short while?

In today's Epistle we are looking at part of a thank-you letter that the apostle Paul wrote to the Philippians. Believe it or not, he was in prison or under house arrest when he wrote, "I have learned in whatever situation I am to be content. I know how to be brought low, and I know how to abound" (Phil 4:11–12). If we are to be content, we have to be prepared to accept both good and bad, often in quick succession. How do we do that?

A woman came to her pastor with a problem that is common but usually is not expressed. Her husband had recently bought a small business. After the first ten months, business blossomed beyond their expectations. "I have a strange feeling. Don't smile at me, but I almost think I should feel guilty."

"Why?" asked the pastor.

"I don't think that we deserve it," she answered, "and I don't think we have earned it."

He thought for a moment and counseled her, "If business is up, thank God. You could sing 'Now thank we all our God.' And when business is down, you could sing the Kyrie, 'Lord, have mercy on us.' God walks with you in both situations."

There are three common ways I have observed in which people try to be content.

"If I make enough money and invest it wisely, I should have more financial security, so at least I won't have to worry about money. Then I can be reasonably content." Few people would argue with that, but financial security is not a secure foundation for contentment. In the parable of the sower, Jesus warned about the danger of "the cares and riches and pleasures of life" choking out our relationship with God (Lk 8:14).

When you think of the pressure of always wanting more, you can understand the popularity of a book like *When All You Have Is Not Good Enough*. It is by an insightful rabbi, Harold Kushner, based on his understanding of Ecclesiastes.

"If I could just think more positively, improve my self-image, be more assertive, and learn how to get other people to do what I want, I would be able to take control of my life, feel good about myself, believe in myself, and achieve what I want. Then I'll be content." But if this is your way of seeking contentment, you must ask, "Can I really change myself for the better?" And other questions arise: "Am I seeking happiness at the expense of others? At what price contentment?"

Some people think they'll be content if they can just escape the whirl of activity and responsibility. "Stop the world; I want to get off." There's too much competition, and it's too confusing. Perhaps they're exhausted. They seek contentment by sitting on the sidelines. But doing so reduces the possibility of sharing God-given gifts and talents with others who need them, and finding the joy that comes from helping others. There is no real contentment in passivity, is there?

I suppose we all have experimented with these options from time to time. But discontentment is a deeply spiritual problem. It afflicts rich and poor alike. We may not want to admit we suffer from it. We may prefer to ignore it. But for most of us it is a recurring problem, eating away at our souls and robbing us of joy.

Yet there is a fourth option—another source of contentment, which is described in our text. Where did the apostle find contentment? In the fact that he was forgiven, justified by God because of Jesus Christ, who died on the cross to forgive all his sins. For this reason, the apostle Paul had peace with God—a peace that surpassed all human understanding, a peace that did not depend in the least upon his circumstances in life.

If we are discontented, it may mean that we have become disconnected from God, that we are not at peace with Him. We are connected to God through faith in His Son. "Since we have been justified by faith, we have peace with God through our Lord Jesus Christ" (Rom 5:1).

We heard in the first part of the Epistle for today, "The peace of God, which surpasses all understanding, will guard your hearts and your minds in Christ Jesus" (v. 7). This peace is not just a mood or something we talk ourselves into. It is the forgiveness and reconciliation with God that Christ has provided at great cost. This peace guards us and protects us. We all need a guardian of peace to accompany us through the twists and turns of life.

Here is what Paul wrote to Timothy about peaceful contentment: "Now there is great gain in godliness with contentment, for we brought nothing into the world, and we cannot take anything out of the world. But if we have food and clothing, with these we will be content. But those who desire to be rich fall into temptation, into a snare, into many senseless and harmful desires that plunge people into ruin and destruction. For the love of money is a root of all kinds of evils. It is through this craving that some have wandered away from the faith and pierced themselves with many pangs" (1 Tim 6:6–10).

The apostle was content because he had learned the sufficiency of God's grace. Do you remember how Paul felt about his "thorn in the flesh?" Three times he pleaded with God to take it away; but the Lord said to him, "My grace is sufficient for you, for My power is made perfect in weakness" (2 Cor 12:9).

The power of God to save is found in the weakness of Christ crucified for us. Paul learned to be content though he often suffered, because he trusted in the Savior who suffered for him. So Paul could say, "Therefore I will boast all the more gladly of my weaknesses, so that the power of Christ may rest upon me. For the sake of Christ, then, I am content with weaknesses, insults, hardships, persecutions, and calamities. For when I am weak, then I am strong" (2 Cor 12:9–10).

This contentment, this inner peace, led him to say, "I can do all things through Him [Christ] who strengthens me" (Phil 4:13). Certain of Christ's gracious presence, His strength enables us to resist temptation, to overcome anger, to forgive, to reach out, to make peace, to outlast evil, to be renewed, to survive, and to love again. "I have learned in whatever situation I am to be content" (Phil 4:11), we heard from the apostle Paul.

One of the most beautiful expressions of Christian contentment came from the pen of the hymn writer Horatio Spafford. He lost his family in a voyage across the Atlantic to Europe. It must have taken great determination and love for him later to make the same voyage. But he came to terms with his God and his grief when he wrote these lines:

> When peace, like a river, attendeth my way;
> When sorrows, like sea billows, roll;
> Whatever my lot, Thou hast taught me to say,
> It is well, it is well with my soul. (*LSB* 763:1)

When the soul finds rest in Christ, there is peace, contentment, and strength to deal with anything life may bring. Having Christ, we have all we will ever need. Peace be with you this Thanksgiving.

Rev. Paul E. Schuessler

Day of National Tragedy

In Remembrance of the Events of September 11, 2001: The First Anniversary

2 Chronicles 7:14

Beloved of Christ Jesus, as we gather for this special service today, let me begin by asking that we not become overly sentimental about this date or use it to feel sorry for ourselves. Rather, our best posture today is to humble ourselves before God and acknowledge that we are always dependant on Him, in good times and bad, in life and in death.

The words I just read from the Old Testament Book of Chronicles were spoken to the nation of Israel, but their New Testament promise is to the Church. God calls us continually (1) to humble ourselves, (2) to pray, (3) to seek His face in the Word and the Sacraments, and (4) to turn from our wicked ways. So may these commands and these promises be the theme for our service today.

Before we get to the matter at hand, let me also welcome members of our Safety Forces here today. We thank God for you! We honor you and pray for you on a regular basis. So when you feel that you are alone and that all things are against you, know that there is a beacon of prayer somewhere in this city, ascending to the King of kings to strengthen, comfort, protect, and defend you. God save and protect you.

Now to the matter at hand—why we're here today: this date marks the one-year anniversary of the boldest terrorist attack in modern history.

It is the single largest act of foreign aggression carried out on American soil since the War of 1812. More people died last year in the terrorist acts of September 11 than at Pearl Harbor.

It was not an act of just war on the part of our enemy; it wasn't self-defense or retribution for wrongs committed against them. Please don't listen to the liberal establishment and other simple-minded people who say that we deserved this or that we brought this upon ourselves because we support Israel as a political ally. Those are only clever lies told by the enemy among us, to divert our attention from what needs to be done.

We've gathered today to contemplate a cold-blooded act of mass murder by people who couldn't sleep at night unless they shed innocent blood. Paul wrote about them 2,000 years ago (Rom 3:15–18) when he said: "Their feet are swift to shed blood: Destruction and misery are in their ways: And the way of peace have they not known."

But this wasn't just an attack on the United States, it was also an attack against Western culture and against the Christian faith that for hundreds of years has inspired and informed Western civilization. And it was carried out against the United States of America because we are the chief representatives of Western life—though we've fallen far from our former glory in that regard.

Radicals, based on what they perceive to be a religious and cultural war in which they want to rule us or destroy us, attacked our government, our economy, and our citizens. Those are the only options for them: rule or destroy. They will never be happy till every woman wears a birkah, every man grows a beard. They want to make music, soccer, television, and flying a kite as illegal here as they were in Afghanistan under the Taliban; and they want every man, woman, and child to bow down to the east five times a day and pray to Allah and to Muhammad.

That's what they want, and it would be impossible to lodge more serious charges against any group of people.

Justice demands that the United States of America (not the Christian Church, but the U.S.A.) strike back with all possible might and that our military forces root out such aggression with all vigor—this is what God established governments for. Without such resolve, civilization ends, tyranny rules, anarchy reigns, the strong only will survive by preying on the weak. There will be no justice, no rights, no peace, no life, no liberty, no pursuit of happiness . . . only a constant state of terror and the most abject slavery as long as people like this go unchallenged.

Such is life in a world whose every inhabitant is incurably infected with sin.

But thanks be to our Lord Jesus Christ who gives us the victory. Although this world will never know very much peace, Jesus overcame sin by His death on the cross and has brought life and immortality to light through the Gospel (2 Tim 1:9). And our Lord's promise is this: that "whoever believes in Him," though he may suffer the worst atrocities in this life, "whoever believes in Him should not perish but have everlasting life" (Jn 3:16).

But there's also something that makes gathering together on this date feel foolish. This is not the greatest calamity ever to strike a people. The bombing of London in World War II was far more tragic than this. The sacking of Constantinople in 1453 was more discouraging than this. In 1932 a man-made famine was responsible for the death of seven million Ukrainian people. And more innocent babies die in abortion chambers each day than died last September.

What feels bad about this gathering is that we've had it so good for so long; we're so ignorant of history as a people and so proud in all the wrong ways that we think we are someone special to have undergone such an attack. We're outraged that someone should do such a thing to us. We think we are entitled to better treatment and should somehow be exempt from such things. But, dear friends, we are no one special.

The history of humanity has been a history of war with a few brief intervals of relative peace and prosperity. And for all of our attempts to create a heaven on earth through so-called "social sciences"—nothing has changed since day one. You and I are as unenlightened and brutal as our forefathers and foremothers thousands of years ago.

And so if we have any reason to gather today may it first be for the sake of humility! Not for prayer—at least not at first. Not to ask God for more goodies so that we can enjoy our prosperity and be left alone to exercise our self-chosen "lifestyle." But for humility's sake, which in Christian terminology means repentance, that is, that we recognize our sins, have sorrow over them, and sincerely confess them to God whom we have offended. Not the imaginary social sins that liberals are always carping about, for there is no such thing—but rather our own personal transgressions against God's Word.

Many of our fellow Americans decry what they consider "immoral" social policy while privately living the most depraved lives imaginable, living in adultery, greedy for gadgets and good times and for personal pleasure, personal fulfillment, personal gain, or the perfect bagel and a cup of cappuccino.

We are a godless and irreverent people, who want freedom without truth, without responsibility and without accountability to anyone, least of all to God. It's true of you and it's true of me; it's true of media anchors and of our nation's schoolteachers; of car mechanics and waitresses. It's the case with retired people and with drug addicts living on the street; with the battered woman and her children too. "All have sinned. . . . None is righteous, no, not one" (Rom 3:23, 10).

Dear friends, we cannot live without Christ, without His grace and mercy and peace, without His love, His Word, and His light in the world to dispel the darkness and the hatred. It all works well in theory, but minus these precious commodities we would all kill one another and die in our sins.

But St. John promises in his first Epistle that "if we confess our sins, [God] is faithful and just to forgive us our sins and to cleanse us from all unrighteousness" (1 Jn 1:9). He proclaims that "we have an advocate with the Father, Jesus Christ the righteous. He is the propitiation for our sins . . . also for the sins of the whole world" (1 Jn 2:1–2).

So let us all humble ourselves before God so that He will exalt us in due time.

It's also important that we meet here today, being led by our own pastors because the past twelve months have encouraged the most incorrect possible ideas about religion.

Some within Christianity have seen this disaster as a call to reject the doctrines that make our holy Christian faith the beacon of hope that it is. Supposed Christians have told us that all religions worship the same God; that the deity of Islam is the same as the one, true God; and that all religions are equally valid before God when they are not.

Christians do not worship the god of Islam. We worship, praise, honor, believe, teach, and confess the Trinity—the Father, Son, and Holy Spirit. And while there are many that men call gods, apart from Him there is no God.

So most important today let us once again consider who God is and what He has done for us. He is the Father who created us, the Son who redeemed us, and the Holy Spirit who sanctifies us in the one true faith.

Dear friends, the Bible teaches, and we believe, that God has created us in His own image! He loves us and sustains us and He has eternal plans for us. We are not accidents. We are not evolved from apes, and we are not alone in this vast universe. We are not hopeless or friendless. We don't only have a God who is the source of all good, but one who reveals Himself in Scripture to be eternal, all-present, all-powerful, all-knowing and most important filled with love and mercy for His fallen creation.

A love shown most perfectly in the sending of His only-begotten Son into the world to redeem us from the sin that has so thoroughly destroyed us. Christ came to be born as we are born; to live and experience all the bitter pain and disappointment of life as you and I do; to take our guilt, our curse, our pain and our penalty upon Himself and to suffer the wages of our sin, to feel icy death and to be forsaken by God, so that we might be eternally received by Him.

"For you know the grace of our Lord Jesus Christ, that, though He was rich, yet for your sakes He became poor, that through His poverty you might be rich" (2 Cor. 8:9).

But God is more than just the Father and the Son; He is also the Holy Spirit who sanctifies us, who causes the Gospel to be preached so that we might hear it and believe. He is the Comforter, the divine Paraclete who puts us in remembrance of all that Jesus did and taught so that we might always have divine Light in our lives. It is He who called us, gathered us, enlightened, and sanctified us by the sacrament of Baptism. It is He who brought the Christian Church into being, against which not even the very gates of hell can prevail, and in which Christian Church He richly and daily forgives the sins of all believers and gives to all believers in Christ everlasting life.

It is He who inspired the Scriptures to be written and called men into the holy ministry to preach them.

It is this same Holy Spirit who has "renewed the face of the earth" by inspiring the noblest of Christian philosophies, which have always stirred men to reach upward and reach outward in love for their fellow man. It is from this very font of Spirit-driven wisdom that mortal man learns mercy and justice, love and sacrifice. And from this firm foundation we have built hospitals, schools, orphanages, and institutions of charitable giving.

This same Holy Spirit has given gifts to men to produce breathtaking works of art and literature which have never been equaled in beauty and in power to inspire; works of Christian liturgy, hymnody, and other great pieces of music that have the power to penetrate our cold hearts and warm them with divine love and mercy, even in our darkest hour.

These things didn't come from Allah or from Muhammad, dear friends. They came from God the Father, God the Son, and God the Holy Ghost.

Don't let anyone confuse you or divert your attention from this only true God and the one saving faith, which only can see you through the greatest trial all of us are yet to face, the storm of death. Through faith in Christ we can die with calm, knowing that our sins have been expunged and that we are beloved children of the heavenly Father, and in whose house are many rooms. Jesus has gone there to prepare one for you; and He will come back to take you there, so that where He is, you may be also.

So give thanks unto the Lord, to the Father, the Son, and the Holy Spirit, for He is good and His mercy endureth forever.

Rev. Dean Kavouras